HOW TO TELL YOUR SKIN TO HEAL ITSELF

Treat your skin conditions emotionally

Dr Pradnya Manwatkar (MBBS, DDVL)

DEDICATION

To my Mom and Dad

ACKNOWLEDGMENTS

This book would not have been possible without the blessings of my parents Prakash and Sanju, the teachings of my dermatology professor Dr V R Sardesai, the guidance of my mentor and teacher - psychiatrist Dr Anand Nadkarni, and the child-like camaraderie I share with my little brother.

1

My Skin Story

The Mirror-on-the-wall was never my friend

Objects in the mirror are cuter than they appear-
said no one ever.
~Anon

Why is a dermatologist, writing a book emphasizing emotions, when it is far too easy to write a book on a 10-step skincare routine, 10-week skin treatment book, quick fixes, or dirty hacks as everyone calls it? Hell, why write at all, when it is easier to prescribe creams, lotions, and shampoos? When there are millions of companies pouring in their monies to get better products? When scientific researchers are working hard to get better, stable, and friendlier creams out into a market that is ripe and ready to believe anything that a company will tell them…?

Why, in the world of such quick fixes, am I, a dermatologist, stuck on to emotional healing?

Because I know that products and treatments don't always give long-lasting results. And because I know what it is to look into the mirror and cry. I know how it feels when someone points out to your face and says, 'your face looks bad', despite having tried all the creams in the world. I know how it feels when people are staring at your acne, rather than looking into your eyes when you are conversing with them, despite having gotten the best of treatments.

My relationship with the Skin started at twelve years of

age when I started getting acne. At first, they started out as a few blackheads and then moved on to become large red raised eruptions. I was told that since my parents had had the issue of acne as teenagers, so would I for a few years, till my pubertal spurt ended. This pubertal spurt, not only started my acne but also did not help me achieve enough height. I was short and overweight for my age, which added to my insecurity about my appearance. Not that I was alone and didn't have friends. Though I was born in Aurangabad I was brought up in Saudi Arabia and it is owing to this wonderful fact that I had friends from different cultures and countries. They were nice people and some of them I am in contact with even today. But I always found myself comparing my skin with theirs. They were like the *Mirror-on-the-wall*, to whom when you asked, 'Who is the fairest of all?', always replied, 'Not you'. But of course, this was all in my head, and in that head of mine, they were always better than me; with their flawless skins and perfect height to body ratio.

After the first year, when my parents realized that my acne was getting worse, they took me to a dermatologist. I used to apply the creams diligently. At twelve years of age, I had grown the maturity to apply the gels the way the dermatologist had explained. I don't remember my mother applying the gels. Not because she didn't care, but because I didn't want her to touch my raw inflamed skin. I wanted to heal myself. I was fiercely independent even then, not by choice, but by the embarrassment that I felt and because I did not want my mother to see my fear. By age thirteen, I was back in the city of my birth and had joined a new school. But I still had acne. Since my dermatologist back in Saudi Arabia wasn't able to help, I thought the next step would be to visit a beauty parlor. Get clean-ups, facials, and steams. Little did I know that it would be an epic failure. But back then I didn't have anyone to tell me any better; Dr. Google had yet to show up and the internet was yet to be flooded with treatment options and recommendations of dermatologists. Years went by and the acne persisted in different intensities. I entered my first year of Medical School with acne. By that time, I was also seeing hints of greying hair, which I again attributed to my genes. It was a frustrating period indeed. As an 18-year-old, the first year of college is exciting. Whether or not you are grown in your minds, you are legally an adult and are prepared to explore the world! The excitement of the first day of college is something I will never forget. However, what I also can never forget is the red acne, which had worsened, in the first month of college. It sucked. Since I was becoming a doctor, I thought it would be prudent to seek treatment from a dermatologist again. This time the treatments worked, and I was elated to see clear skin. But there was agony to come when I heard my friend say those dreaded words, 'You have scars.' I remember going home and checking the scars out in the mirror and feeling devastated. The mirror-on-the-wall stared back at me. I had won the battle, but my war was yet to begin.

Years went on. My acne mellowed down, but the scars remained not only on my skin but on my confidence. Yet, I was constantly holding up a façade to show the world how confident I was. So good was I at hiding my insecurity, that years later, I was told by many acquaintances, that I came across as a snob. This insecurity about my appearance harboured a do-or-die attitude. I tried hard to excel in anything that I touched. Be it being a doctor, an actor, or a painter, I had to be the best or it wasn't enough. Anything less than good wasn't a big enough compensation for my acne and scars. Today, as I retrospectively analyze the past years, it was an exhausting time indeed.

Circa 2009 is when I started my clinical practice and that is the year when my acting career also picked up. I like to thank my stars that I got this lucky break and met the right kind of people to work with. From 2009 till 2017, I had done multiple plays with the stalwarts of the theatre world like Pandit Satyadev Dubey, TV commercials with the most renowned production houses, starred in two Marathi movies as the lead actress, and also performed as Miss Mala in the Hindi film *Jagga Jasoos* which was directed by none other than Anurag Basu! I was living the high life. I still had scars, but the fake facade of confidence was good enough to camouflage the insecurity that rested behind them. But as someone said all good things come to an end, mine did too. One day I got up with shoulder spasm so severe that it left me bedridden for days and in pain for the next several months. I was diagnosed with a condition called *acute trapezitis.*

The pain was intense and radiated from my right shoulder to the right side of my head, leading to headaches that were no less than an attack of migraine. No amount of aspirin or painkillers helped in those attacks. My uncle, who is an orthopaedician, told me to take rest and physiotherapy. He attributed the attack to my travel on the local train. I was working in a hospital at the time, to learn and get trained in cosmetic dermatology. I used to leave my house at 8 am, reach work at 9 am, and work till 6 pm, post which I used to run my clinic between 7 pm to 9 pm. Not to forget, I used to find time for shoots and drama rehearsals as well. And not once did I complain. It was the primetime of my life, in which I was living on my own volition, with no rules at all. The purse that I carried on my right shoulder, and my constant travel back and forth from work, was probably what had injured the shoulder muscle. Considering the nature of the injury, I should have recovered in a month, at the most two months. But I continued to suffer over the next two years and lo behold, it did not stop there. To add to my agony, I got an attack of acne, again.

Imagine my plight- I was now an actor and a dermatologist - with acne. My directors and cameramen noticed and so did my patients. I recall how a patient once told me on my face 'I won't get treated by you because it seems you can't treat yourself.' It was embarrassing and heart-breaking. My acne, in my mind of course, was proving to be a measuring scale for my talent, success, and kindness. The shoulder pain was now chronic and once it led to my headaches nothing worked. I always had to sleep it off.

One day, after about two years of pain, I finally exploded like a volcano and met my uncle with the attitude of a Ninja, not ready to back down till he helped me get rid of this pain for good. He had assumed since I hadn't complained to him about the pain, that my shoulder ache was done and dusted years ago. That's when he asked me a question that challenged the way I was living my life till then - 'What stress do you have?'

I looked at him with eyes wide enough to fly out of my sockets onto his examination table. Here I was living the life of a doctor and an actor in the city of dreams called Mumbai. I was independent and I was happy or so I thought before this question was posed. The only thing that I was unhappy or displeased about was that I wasn't making 'enough' money to live comfortably. I was making enough to pay the bills, but not enough to say — 'I'll drive my Porsche instead of the Jaguar today.' Yes, I was 'struggling', not to put bread on my table, but to buy a car of my choice or run off on a vacation to my dream destination. At the time it seemed valid. I was at an age where I attributed my success to only owning fancy cars, traveling in first-class, and wearing fancy jewellery... rather anything fancy. Plus, my need to compensate for my acne and scars was proving to be the catalyst for me to do more, to be 'enough' in my own eyes. Somehow, I had come to think that all fancy materialistic things would be a good compensation for not having fancy flawless skin.

In short, the cover of my book was exciting, but the story was mediocre. However, my compensatory mechanism was so strong, that people around me seemed to think I had it all! I made my life seem flawless. And the funniest part was that I made it appear flawless to *me*. I had convinced myself that these struggles are a part and parcel of life. That everyone goes through them. That if you didn't have one thing, something else could compensate for it. Little did I know that I was lying to myself. And these lies were causing stress thereby leading to my chronic shoulder pain, headaches, and now my acne. My uncle suggested a 10-day course of a drug called amitriptyline. There was some resistant at first to take the same. That a doctor needed anti-anxiety medicine seemed silly to me. Plus, I was in a state of pure evil denial that I was stressed and in need of a drug to curb my anxiety. But due to my obsession to 'be enough', I did go ahead with the medicine and lo behold, a simple 10-day course of amitriptyline worked like magic. The shoulder pain that had plagued me for over a little more than 2 years had completely disappeared.

Like one question challenged the way I was living my life, my recovery changed my perspective towards life. I realized how much anxiety is a part of our lives and how good we all have become at hiding it, not from the world, but ourselves. Stress was now being categorized into 'little', 'some' and 'lots', and 'to be a little stressed' was the new normal. I was a glaring example of how stress had slithered in like the snake from Harry Potter into my chamber of secrets. Here I was a doctor who knew with certainty that stress was a silent killer leading to diabetes and strokes, and still hadn't been able to even identify it in my life. Ironically, such good an actor was I, that I had managed to fool myself for years.

As soon as I accepted this fact, I started identifying it in people around me. Years of leg ache my mother suffered, the years of migraine my friend suffered, the submucous fibrosis my grandmother suffered, all made sense. These weren't just physical manifestations, but they were somatic manifestations of psychological stress on their bodies. When my patients complained, I listened carefully than ever before. All those flares of atopic dermatitis, acne, hair fall, psoriasis, and vitiligo that would not go away with years of treatment, started to make sense. Stress had become a pandemic. It was everywhere. And as for me, although I had identified my stress triggers and used to abort my attacks of shoulder pain very effectively, it wasn't enough. The pain showed its ugly head now and again so did the acne. So, in November of 2017, I enrolled myself in a self-help workshop in Rational Emotive Behaviour Therapy (REBT). And the one single formula that REBT offered changed my life. One single formula.

Right from getting challenged in the way I was living my life, to changing my perspective towards life, to restructuring my life completely, was a journey that I had never imagined I would take. Such realizations and paths were meant for Yogi's — not me. But here I was, a living breathing example of how life could make a full 180 degree turn for the better. My acne had indeed proven to be a catalyst for me towards realizing that I was living a life on an auto-mode. It had proven to be a catalyst for me to look beyond what I could see. Finally, in January of 2018, I started studying REBT, at the Institute of Psychological Health, headed by Dr Anand Nadkarni, so that I could pass on this information to all those who wanted to look beyond what they were seeing in their lives.

From the moment I started the practice of Emo-dermatology (as I like to call it), till today, I get patients with skin diseases who are frustrated or terrified. Diseases like psoriasis and vitiligo can ruin lives. And I have seen patients cry and hurt over why they aren't 'normal' . I have seen girls scared because they aren't 'fair' enough. I have seen mothers fuss over their daughter's hair because it isn't thick enough. I also realized, that even if I did pander to the demands of my patients for fair skin and hair and gave good treatment outcomes, they still ended up back at my office with recurrences, at a later date, or they ended up going to another dermatologist who was most likely to prescribe the same medicines albeit in a different combination. I have realized that prescribing medicines and creams alone is not going to work at all. A change in the emotional quotient is needed as well. Keeping this in mind, I felt I had to do something more. And this something more has translated into this book.

Through this book, I pass on the baton to heal your skin yourself. A simple formula that when used effectively, will not only help your dermatologist give you results but help you keep the disease at bay.

I will confess, however, as much as I am getting good at dealing with my stress, I still have days when I struggle, I still get acne here and there, and a headache on and off. The Slytherin snake called Stress is relentless with a long life. But I know, with the use of REBT, I will get better at jabbing the sword of Gryffindor into its deadly jaw and killing it. I will have evolved my emotional quotient a little more. At least to the level that nothing affects me. To the level that the Mirror-on-the-wall stays a mirror and nothing more.

Dr Albert Ellis rightly says, *"If you stop, really stop, damning yourself, others, and unkind conditions, you would find it almost impossible to upset yourself emotionally- about anything. Yes, anything."*

It is always the journey that matters in the Now. Nothing else matters. And when you master your journey, nothing will ever upset you.

So, for all those on board… let us begin this journey because you are in for a ride of a lifetime!

And for those who still feel that only creams work, go ahead and see how you couldn't be further away from the truth.

2

Only creams don't work!
YOU make them work

People have motives and thoughts of which they are unaware
~Dr Albert Ellis

Ask for what you want and be prepared to get it
~ Maya Angelou

S top using creams!

Yes, you read me right. If you have been using over-the-counter (OTC) products or dermatologist recommended creams for years and haven't gotten a great result, then stop using creams… And read this book.

And if the answer to *any* of the following questions is YES, then you *need* to read this book.

1. Have you been to many dermatologists and have seen minimal or no results?
2. Have you followed the advice of your favorite superstar and bought all sorts of recommended products and still seen no change in your skin?
3. Have you seen fantastic results after using creams, but the skin dulls each time you stop using them?
4. Do you have adult acne that suddenly occurred out of nowhere?
5. Do you have early greying of hair?
6. Do you have psoriasis that puts you in an embarrassing situation at work or even at home?

7. Have you suffered from hair fall that you fear will turn into baldness?
8. Have you suffered from vitiligo and have no idea how you got it because no one in your family had it?
9. Have you felt your skin dulling and making you look older than you are, despite using the best creams?

And the most important question:

10. Smile, if anyone has called you uncle or aunty when they should've called you Bro or *Didi**? *(And now imagine me smiling. Because I have been called an aunty when I was a mere twenty-five.)*

I suppose we all have been in awkward situations, where we felt older, unattractive, or simply unhealthy because of our skin.
The biggest and the most visible organ of our body tends to fail us now and again. It tends to make us feel vulnerable more often than not.

Let's play a game. Read and follow the instructions below:

Imagine a wonderfully ripe Orange, Mango, or pineapple (or any food of your choice). Remember the taste, the texture, the smell, and how it felt on your tongue.
Now close your eyes and imagine. Go on… Try it. It's my sincere attempt to explain a vital connection between the brain and the organs, which we so often miss.

What happened?
The usual response would be salivation!

When we think of food (a thought in the brain), our brain creates an image of that fruit in our mind's eye. This image stimulates the same nerves that would have been stimulated if you would have seen, smelled, and touched the fruit in real time. This image caused a physical response on the tongue despite the absence of that food!

Here, the parasympathetic nervous system was working in full swing. What is this garbled language you ask? Let me simplify it for you.

The parasympathetic nervous system is one part of the autonomic nervous system (ANS). The other part of the ANS is the sympathetic nervous system. This ANS is like an unending entangled web of wires running all through your body, carrying tiny electric currents. You could call them your personalized electric wires. The sympathetic nervous system causes a state of acceleration- like an increase in heart rate, extra sweating, fast breathing, etc. And the parasympathetic nervous system acts like a break by reducing the heart rate, sweating, and the breathing.

And guess what, you have met these two systems before. Rather you meet them every day when you breathe, digest food, and poop. It is this ANS that is helping you breathe in air and digest your food without you even knowing it! There is a constant flow of triggers happening between the ANS, your thoughts, and the various organs in your body like your heart, lungs, intestines, tongue, etc., and even the skin. Ever wonder why you breathe? Or how your heart beats? Even the salivation in the example above, was the result of a biofeedback between your thought in the brain, the ANS, and tongue.
This feedback is what enables all routine activities of your body and brain to function in harmony.

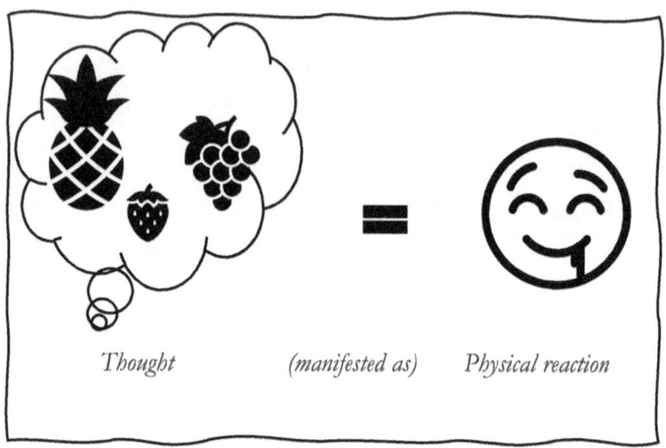

Figure- 2.1 Body- Brain Feedback

Which means, if thoughts were an intricate part of the biofeedback, then could it be that these thoughts, pleasing (positive) and harmful (negative), could be influencing the physical nature of our being in real time?

Confused? Here are a few more questions I have for you:

1. Have you had huge acne on your face a day before your exam?
2. Have you had to rush to the toilet right before a speech?

And this one is my favorite:

3. Have you felt butterflies in your tummy when you saw the love of your life?

If you have answered *yes*, then know that it is these entangled bunch of wires in the ANS and your thoughts which have triggered your organs in manifesting- acne before an exam, a toilet run before your speech, and the fluttering of your heart when you saw your love.

All thoughts can manifest, rather *do manifest* as physical

reactions of your body in real time. Some may be evident, as the ones mentioned above, and some not as much. The ones that aren't evident can only be detected when too late- like when you get vitiligo or psoriasis or blood pressure. This should pose a very important question: Could we then manage our thoughts so that we could get better or healthier physical responses? Could we voluntarily think pleasing thoughts and get a glowing skin? Yes! We could and we do more often than not.

 A pleasing thought of your loved one is bound to put a smile on your face, leading to a reduction in your frown lines! Unfortunately, it isn't the pleasing thoughts that cause the problem. The harmful or negative thoughts, commonly referred to as Automatic Negative Thoughts or ANT's are the issue. Like ants occur in millions and are very perseverant… so are our ANT's. And why are they called automatic? Because, if you had the choice, if anyone had a choice, would you want to think a positive pleasing thought that made you smile, or would you like to think a negative thought that made you seethe in anger or sadness?
Pleasing thoughts make you happy and feel loved. These too are generated automatically but are often taken for granted and not enjoyed. The ANT's, however, are the ones we tend to fight hard against, giving them more importance than what should have been given. ANT's continue to have negative physiological/physical response in the form of various skin diseases. Even a common and seemingly mundane condition like acne can be a negative manifestation of an ANT/ harmful thought.

Now here is some food for thought:
Louise L Hay says, *'If we want a joyous life, we must think joyous thoughts. If we want a prosperous life, we must think prosperous thoughts. If we want a loving life, we must think loving thoughts. Whatever we send out mentally or verbally will come back*

to us in like form."
I want to add to this and say: If we want healthy skin, rid of
diseases, then we must think healthy thoughts. We must change our
negative thoughts to positive ones if we are to expect the creams that
we apply to create magic and heal our skin!"

Thus, I proclaim, that only creams don't work: *You* make
them work.

This book is my small way of trying to pass on to you my
experiences as a dermatologist. It is my way of bringing to
your notice that when your body and mind are unhealthy,
your skin is unhealthy too. And it is my way of telling you
that unless you deal with the way you *think*, your skin will
never behave in the way you want it to.

Sounds complicated? Don't worry, I am here to make it
simple.
But before we begin, a teeny-weeny disclaimer: If you have
picked up this book thinking you will see some miraculous
10-step skincare regime or 6-week skin transformation
tips, then you might want to put it back. This book ain't
for the weak-hearted. But shall I dare say, it is for the
thick-skinned.

If you're still holding on to this book let's begin…

3

HOW to read this book
*By re-setting your Emotion= **Energy in Motion***

What you think, you become
~Gautam Buddha

I think therefore I am
~René Descartes

As I said, I have tried to keep it simple. But being the largely diligent and overtly obsessive 'information giving' doctor that I am in my clinic, I have added at the end of this book, the basic structure of the skin, because *if you don't understand a subject well enough, you can't use the information well enough.* As I say, *Basic-Mein-Rada (BMR)** is a No-No! You could go brush up your knowledge on skin or continue to read the subsequent chapters in line.

I see the skin in its myriad of presentations, and not only related to cosmesis. With all of them causing distress to the person suffering, I could not limit myself to writing a book only on facial skin or what we commonly know as cosmetic dermatology.

Plus, because of my personal emotional journey battling with acne, I am a firm believer of psychosomatic medicine that led me to study a form of psychotherapy called Rational Emotive Behaviour Therapy (REBT) which I incorporate in my daily practice. I not only deal with the pathology that the skin presents with but also the psychological changes that the patient undergoes because of the pathology. And, as much as it seems underrated or understated or even over-

15

** Trouble in understanding*
the basics of a subject

-simplified, it is not.

The amount of psychological trauma that condition like a zits or hair thinning can cause is enough to last a lifetime. Those who have gone through skin conditions would know exactly what I am talking about. I see people getting sucked in the whirlpool of harmful thoughts about their skin and hair diseases. There is a lot of frustration that furthers these negative thoughts, and the cycle continues. Most of the time, this frustration is because of thoughts like '*How the world will see me*', and other times it's because of the '*Why me*' question they ask themselves.

But, as I mentioned in the previous chapter, the amount of psychological trauma/ harmful thoughts that can lead to manifestations of skin diseases also needs to be understood. Yes, as much as a skin disease can cause you psychological trauma, a disturbed psychology due to harmful thoughts could have probably been the reason why your skin disease manifested in the first place.

But remember *Fig. 2.1*? Thoughts lead to physical manifestations. So let us move ahead and study the flow chart below:

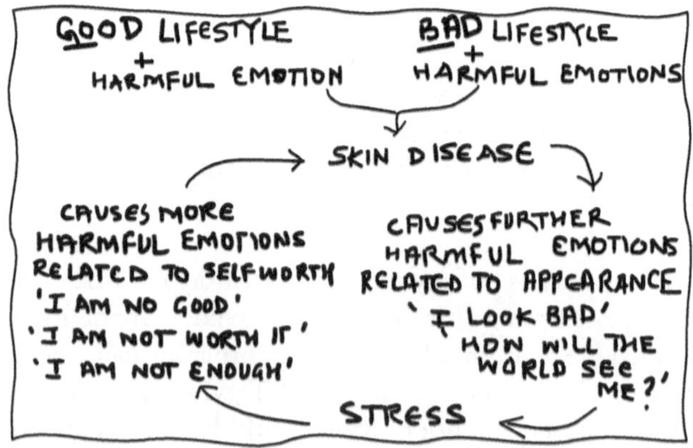

Figure 3.1- The vicious cyle of negative emotions (stress) and skin diseases

If you look at the flow chart, the skin disease happened because of a harmful thought *unrelated* to the skin disease, and this skin disease further led to harmful thoughts aggravating the skin disease. Do you see how vicious this circle is? Lifestyle also matters as much. If you haven't had a healthy lifestyle, you see that it increases the chances of skin diseases in you. And funnily, even if you had a good lifestyle but you were unable to regulate or manage your harmful thoughts you would still manifest the skin disease. Because your skin is not only regulated by your actions but also by your thoughts. It is an entire organ system and it functions in a very systematic manner taking in multiple inputs as a computer takes in and creating multiple complex outputs at the same time. This flow chart is an indicator that in order to have a sustainably healthy and glowing skin you would have to approach your skincare and skin treatments in a holistic manner.

An important truth that I have learned over the years of my practice is this: We take the biggest and the most vulnerable organ of our body, that which protects us from the heat, cold, sun, wind, rain, bacteria, viruses, fungi, and even cancer, for granted. We will abuse it with creams, cosmetics, treatments, experimental remedies, and even voodoo. But we won't try and understand its needs and the messages it conveys. We won't see it as intricate organ system and understand the feedback it gives us.

No one is to be blamed; I sailed the same boat. We grow up seeing our parents, people, and friends in our environment like schools, colleges, and our neighbors. We see movies and read books, and yet, we never see any emphasis given to the skin. Imagine, the hero or heroine getting up and applying her day-care cream and the movie starts? We are influenced, even motivated, by these very hero's and heroine's when we see them exercise in a movie. We want to go to the Tomatina festival when we see Hrithik, Abhay, and Farhan enjoy it. We want to do exactly what the trio did in the Hindi film *Zindagi Milegi na Dobara*.

What if the three shared a sunscreen in the open roof car, or if Hrithik was shown as having psoriasis and applied his skin cream—I am sure everyone would want to do the same.

In the word of Gautam Buddha: '*What you think you become*'. And I dare add to this and say that what you *see* around you is also what you become. The constant influence of our environment, people, media, and the internet, is leading us to believe that a certain ' Saffron based' cream can make you fair, that a certain ZPTO shampoo is enough to treat dandruff, that a PRO V shampoo can arrest hair fall, (and this is my favorite) that 'herbal' remedy can make a bald man grow hair. Here I want to shout out loud, at the top of my lungs, that if it were so simple, us breed of dermatologists would cease to exist. But we do exist, and we will continue to exist for the simple reason that the skin is an intricate organ and treatments need to be holistically driven. Period.

The fingertip generation (as I call it); the one that gets everything done at the tip of the finger on the mobile, has seemed to fallen prey to this thinking the most. And this has led to worsening of beliefs like quick fix creams, 15-day miracle cures, hair fixes, etc. And more such 'magical' creams continue to pour into the market.

Our thoughts haven't been more detrimental to us than they are today. And as much as creams matter, so does changing harmful thoughts. It is high time we stopped taking everything at face value and started asking the tough questions:

1. Are randomly occurring harmful negative thoughts or ANT's, responsible for the manifestation of the skin disease?
2. How can we change these negative thoughts permanently?

We need to start inculcating the thought that our skin is

a part of our body. Its beauty and health will be long lasting only if we make our bodies and minds healthy. Not one cream. Not one regime. But a customized and holistic approach that includes creams, regimes, and changing your thoughts.

Changing thoughts is an intimidating process and at this juncture I make a candid confession: I still struggle with my thoughts. Another confession I would like to make: As you start feeling a sense of mastery over them, when you feel you are getting good at identifying thoughts and making sense of them, is when your bubble of belief bursts and you get a taste of reality… Why am I confessing this now? I got a taste of reality a while ago. My confidence as a dermatologist and my thought that I was getting good at helping my patients was challenged by my patient Mr S.

The accusation that he made is something I can never forget. Thus, here is my last confession: My thought process about the world of dermatology and healing the skin changed forever…

4

The Circuit Of Logic That Mr S Lost
The day I failed as a Dermatologist

From anger, delusion arises and from delusion bewilderment of learning. When learning is bewildered, intelligence is lost, and when intelligence is lost, one falls again into the material pool.
~6.23 Bhagavad Gita

"You cannot help me!" said Mr S said with rage.

My smile turned to a look of shock. My bright lovely consulting room, lined with white-washed walls, turned grey. The air conditioner was throwing flames of fire. The drops of sweat that appeared on my upper lip made the makeup I wore pointless. My perfume made me gag and the fancy bracelet I wore transformed into handcuffs put on by the police. My favorite fountain pen that I was holding, as I always do when a patient is speaking, felt like Thor's hammer.

"Then why are you here?" I muttered thinking if his behavior was at all appropriate. Scenes of angry mobs vandalizing hospitals flashed in my mind. At some point, many doctors in private practice face the brunt of patient anger. But the patients that I had encountered in my practice were decent and understanding. This gentleman, however, was a glaring antithesis.

His face grew red as he spoke, so much so, that it seemed even his psoriasis had gone scalier to prove how bitter he was. This ruddy-faced bald man reeked of anger, an anger which he had misdirected towards me. He had been to multiple dermatologists, all of whom had managed to control his psoriasis, but only for a short period. The disease continued to show its ugly head now and again and that added to his frustration. The psoriasis would flare around important events like weddings and parties, causing him a lot of social embarrassment. The white cap that he wore on his head, which had turned yellow and tattered, was like the crown of shame for him which he kept adjusting so that he could hide his eyes behind its rim as he spoke these harsh words of condemnation.

"I am here because of my friend's insistence," he said pulling his cap further down his face to cover his eyes. "You are the last dermatologist I am ever going to meet if your treatment doesn't work." A stream of sweat ran down the side of his neck stopping at his collar bone.

I stared at him with a fake stoicism. Shouting back at a patient would be akin to murder in my fraternity. Ignoring him would make me seem too weak. Silence would be like admitting he was right. The red color on my face was starting to match the red color on his face, with the avalanche of emotions that he had incited in me.

I heard my Mother's words ring in my ears, *'Smile if you don't know what to say.'* Taking a deep breath and putting on the best smile my face allowed me I said, "What if I told you that you did not need a dermatologist to heal your psoriasis?"

It was his turn to look at me with shock. He tilted his head upwards and peered from under the rim of his cap. For the first time, his eyes made contact with mine, albeit for a brief moment. Those same eyes were all over the place, shifting focus on everything that was there in the room, as if experiencing a bout of nystagmus. A wave of triumph overcame me. The color of my face was getting back its brown tint.

"What— ?" He mumbled under his breath, unsure of what he had heard was right. He took out a handkerchief from his pocket to wipe out the puddle of sweat around his collar bone. I could now see his full face that hid under the rim of his cap. His expressions had seemed to ease out. The stiffness in his body had started to give away.

"You heard me right. There is one single formula that can help heal your psoriasis, but you need to show some trust in the process," I stated stolidly. "I am afraid, if you are here because a friend asked you to be here, then I recommend that you see some other doctor." I picked up the fountain pen to write down a few names that came to mind. "Some of my colleagues have a wonderful healing hand." I looked at him and smiled harder. Believe me, no matter how bitter I was at his outburst, the dermatologist in me wanted to accept this challenge he had thrown at me; of helping him when no one else could.

The silence in the room was audible. His eyes had steadied and he kept staring at the wet and crumpled handkerchief. "Okay." He finally announced.

I heaved a sigh of relief as well and started examining him. The red patches were thick and seen everywhere on his body. The flakes that flew off his skin, had settled down on the examination bed, creating a lake of scales. He tried hard to sweep them off the bed. His shame was as intense as that of a man caught red-handed in the middle of an act of perversion.

As he spoke with great animation about the disease that had plagued him over the pasts twenty years, I realized his pent-up frustration. I stopped examining him and decided to only listen. He had years of agony to share. "Thanks for hearing me out," he said. I looked up at him to see a hint of a smile on his face. A glimmer of hope as I would call it.

As I started to write down the prescription, I could see his expression change back to angst. "But you said I could heal this myself. What is the single formula? Is this some kind of ruse to get me to feel hope, like a placebo effect?"

"Not at all," I retorted with patience. "I will tell you the single formula when you come the next time."

He shifted in his seat with unease. His anger was making a comeback.

"Do you know Surdas?" I asked withholding the secret formula that I had. "Surdas was a blind saint. He wanted to learn all about God and Spirituality. He approached a Guru and requested to be his disciple. But Surdas had anger issues and he was infamous for them. The Guru refused to take him as a disciple. Can you guess why?" Mr. S's eyes fixed on my face as I was talking. He nodded his head sideways.

"Was he rude with the Guru?" he asked.

"No, he wasn't. He was the most humble and polite version that he could be. Yet, the Guru asked him to chant the name of God and come back after a month." I had Mr S's full attention now. "Surdas accepted this homework and for a month chanted the name of God, day in and day out. After thirty days, as he walked with joy to his Guru's hut, a sweeper by accident soiled his clothes. He went wild with rage, yelling at the sweeper, but continued his journey to his Guru's home. *Go back and chant the name of God for another month,* said the Guru to Surdas's surprise. When Surdas asked why he had to repeat this task, the Guru said nothing. Surdas, a little dejected went back and continued to chant the name of God for another month. As he walked to his Guru's home for the second time, the sweeper soiled his clothes again, and as expected Surdas couldn't let go of his anger. The Guru asked him to chant the name for another month. Surdas was desperate to learn from this Guru, and so chanted for another month. That day, as he walked to the Guru's home, the sweeper soiled his clothes for the third time. But this time Surdas did not yell. He bent his head and said, *Thank you for teaching me how to control my anger. I understand it is not your fault that you soiled my clothes but a mere accident that happened.* That day the Guru accepted him as his disciple. "Why do you think the Guru wanted him to chant the name of God?" Mr. S sat in silence as I continued, "Because chanting made his mind calm. The anger that had caused his outburst would subside and only a mind which is calm is capable of logical reasoning and thinking. This part of the brain that allows logical thinking is lost when the person is angry, sad, or anxious. I like to call it the Circuit of Logic and Surdas's Circuit of Logic needed rebooting. He needed to have a calm mind to be able to process any information or wisdom the Guru was going to teach him."

Mr S sat up straight and adjusted the rim of his cap so that he could see my face better.

"Anger is one emotion that clouds our logical thinking. Fortunately, anger is only a tendency, and this tendency can be changed. It is not a fixed personality trait, as most of us assume. It is but a mere habit that has formed through years of nature, nurture, and culture, that leads to one's unique personality or signature is called. And when we get angry, we cannot think right. And when we can't think straight, we can't comprehend new information or trust the information that is being given. So, if Surdas wanted to learn a new thing, he needed to change his thinking habits, so that healthy thinking habits could be sown and grown for newer information to be processed. New habits of patience, kindness, and most importantly of trust. He needed to achieve a calmer state if mind in order to process any what the Guru was to teach. It is a slow process Mr S, and like Surdas couldn't think with logic because of his tendency towards anger, I doubt if you knowing this formula today will do you any good."

He continued to listen intently. "Angry people are like *chakri** bombs ready to explode. You can't stop a *chakri* bomb unless it made its round by using up all the gun powder. Try to diffuse a *chakri* bomb and see what happens. That is how angry people function. They aren't thinking with logic. I call it the Circuit of Logic. This circuit that is responsible for logical thinking, which is present in the frontal part of your brain, has shorted. Like a fuse short-circuits." I tried to gauge from his expressions if he understood what I was explaining. "How many times have you seen people on the roadside trying to pacify other angry people in a mob? The angry men in the mob are like a bunch of Bahubali's, trying to right the wrong. They continue to

A firecracker that twirls on the floor in fast circular motion

vandalize or fight and will stop only when they start *thinking* with *logic,* that is when their Circuit of Logic reboots itself. Till then, the people on the roadside, the spectators, have to wait for the mob's anger to settle down."

Mr S seemed lost in thought. He was playing with the crumpled handkerchief in his hand with his head bowed low. "I am sorry," he said meekly.

"I am not here to make you feel bad. My job is to help you. And like I had asked you to trust me, you need to trust the process as well Mr S. Can you do that?" I asked with complete sincerity. "Let's start with the treatment. Let me understand your skin and I will give you time to understand how the creams function. Without trust, there can be no improvement, even if I gave you the secret this very instant. And like the mob, we need to refresh our Circuit of Logic. Both of us need to do that."

He continued to look at his hands as I continued to write his prescription. The friction of the pen against the paper penetrated the icy silence.

"I cannot guarantee anything doctor," he finally said with uncertainty. "I will follow this prescription and see how it goes. I will come back only if these creams work."

My heart sank… Anger is one of the biggest roadblocks a person can face. And the only way to overcome this block is through perseverance by the individual who feels the anger. I couldn't do anything more for him at that point in time. His Circuit of Logic needed to get rebooted. I handed over the prescription, hoping to see him after fifteen days.

Let me be completely honest. I have always dreaded this particular type of patient, who comes in and word bullies you. Yes, doctors get scared too. At least I do. As much I was angry at his outburst, I was frightened as well. This hadn't been an easy interaction for me, but at the same time, I was aware that as a doctor I needed to be empathetic. My Circuit of Logic needed a reboot as well. And what better way than meeting the Crazy Five! How I thanked my stars that evening that I was about to meet them for dinner. My five crazy friends who made my crazy life less crazy!

5

The Crazy Five And The Single Formula That No One Listened To

The A+B= C of Skincare

*We cannot change anything until we accept it. Condemnation does
not liberate, it oppresses.*
~Carl Jung

The only normal people are the ones who don't know very well
~Alfred Adler

I looked at the watch. It was 7.30 pm and I was late for my party. I come from a small historically rich city called Aurangabad where I attended school and met the Crazy Five. We did make time to meet, but we had lost touch over the past year. Today's party was an arduously planned event, and no matter how broken my Circuit of Logic was, I wasn't going to let it come in the way of the joyous evening that beckoned me over. I knew the Crazy Five would lighten my spirits in no time.

I was the second last to arrive at the restaurant. It was a beautiful, well-lit space, with fairy lights and old-fashioned furniture. The occasional waft of the focaccia bread was proving to be elating. The clanking of the plates with spoons created a symphony that made my heart sing.

"Hey!" shouted Payal, Crazy no. 1, from the far end, a successful banker working in Singapore. She was a tall woman and with her flawless brown skin, auburn eyes, and athletic body, she always stood out. I waved back to this beauty and joined the table.

"Hey, Champa Chameli*! You look as if someone beat you," blurted Crazy no. 2 Varun, addressing me with a nickname he had kept for me. He was an electrical engineer who was on the verge of selling his third startup. This success oozed from him as I looked at the towering bear-like but handsome buffoon. Here was a good-looking man with a great zest for life and the joker of the lot too. He was the risk-taker, the 'Business Tycoon' as we joked, and the charmer as well, now married with two beautiful children. But who could stop a charmer, a good-looking one at that, from being one.

"Hi, Handsome!" I winked at him as I grabbed a drink from off the table.

"That's mine!" yelled Mira, no. 3 of the Crazy Five, a pretty petite woman, with dark and curly hair. She was the Mother Hen of our group. Kind and caring with a heart the size of a jumbo jet. That humongous heart of hers had a place for everyone. It was as if she was incapable of feeling wrath for anyone that walked this planet, even if she wanted to. To her, everyone was nice, but circumstances made them unkind. Forgive and forget was her mantra. She had given her career up in the field of music to take care of her family and by far was excelling at being the best mother, wife, daughter, and daughter-in-law- not to forget. 'Her voice is like butter,' my mother used to say. And there never was a reunion where we did not ask her to sing our favorite melodies. Paying no heed to her I said, "You order another one for you."

"What happened?" chimed Nihar. This crazy no. 4 was the black sheep, not only in his family but also in my school. With his long hair tied in a bun at the top of his head and a braided goatee, he looked like he would be undergoing

*A name, but in this case
term of endearment*

*sanyas** at any moment. He had gone on to learn about agriculture and had become a successful farmer/ entrepreneur/ rebel/ socialist. Trying to bridge the gap in all the social injustice that happened with farmers, animals, birds, and the environment, he was our Greta Thunberg. And yes, he was creating a buzz already.

And here I was, graduated as a dermatologist and was now running her clinic in Mumbai, a place that was alien to her, getting yelled at by patients. I had had my set of failures and successes as a doctor, but today's experience surpassed all precedents. My frustration of 'not doing enough for my patients' multiplied due to this episode. I gulped down the Sangria in one go and gave a weak smile. The makeup that had run off during my sweating spree with Mr S couldn't hide my tiredness.

"What has happened?" everyone yelled in unison. I ended up narrating the entire interaction like a professional actor. I could have gotten an Oscar for my portrayal of emotions and put to shame all the Meryl Streep's of the world.

"I like this Mr S," exclaimed Nihar. "He wasn't wrong with what he said."

I looked at him with complete disgust. My award-winning performance hadn't incited an ounce of empathy from this goatee bearded-due-to-become-a-*sanyasi*** fellow. "How can you say that?" I yelled.

"Yes, he was rude, but what he said is a fact." Said Payal in a pragmatic business-like tone.

I was like a sheep cornered by a pack of wolves. "What about you Mira? Do you think this patient was right?" I asked Mother Hen, seeking some solace.

"I had an aunt who had psoriasis, and she died with it. She had been to so many dermatologists. All those medicines helped her but only till she used the medicines. The moment she stopped the psoriasis always came back. She gave up over the years, as I recall," her voice trailed off for a moment. "I think this patient wasn't right at yelling at you, but I do understand his frustration towards doctors," said Mira finally, looking me in the eye.

My sweaty beaded lip was in full form by now. People could have mistaken my sweat for Swarovski crystals, that's how bright the sweat shined.

"My sister had… wait… still has an acne issue at age thirty-three!" said Varun. "And she can get upset about it. I have seen her crib on and on about all the 'hundred doctors' she has been to, allopathy or otherwise. The other day she ended up applying raw aloe gel all over her face and burst into a rash. Seems she visited Dr. Google this time!"

Everyone laughed but me. I was hapless. Forget any word of solace for me, no one had uttered a word of gratefulness even towards my profession. "Are you all saying that dermatologists don't help as much?" I uttered with exasperation.

"And what do you think dermatologists do?" blurted Raghav. He was the last, crazy no. 5, to join. Everyone turned towards him, and I did too with a hint of irritation.

"Hey Raghav," said everyone, excluding me. I was already on the defense and here was Raghav adding to my woes.

"All of them are happy being cosmetologists these days! Aren't you?" he laughed and sat next to me.

Raghav was the second doctor among us. And by a doctor, I mean he was pitched to be the fastest upcoming Cardiac Surgeons of our generation. Tall with boyish looks, a smooth voice, and a lean body, he carried an aura of success around him. With his impeccable dressing sense, he was hard to ignore. Unfortunately for me though, he never seemed to warm up to the notion that we as doctors were on the same team. To think that I should have gotten some support from him was like saying Harry and Voldermort were best of friends. "It is a great business to be in – become a cosmetologist and run a chain of cosmetic centres. You get the best of both worlds- being a doctor and earning at the same time," said he.

I am so used to hearing such statements that I have realized arguing only makes me (and us as a fraternity of dermatologists) look guilty. And ignoring Raghav was a better tactic as far as my experience went. I knew him since our post-graduate days and the single most effective way to shut him up was to shut up yourself. Silence speaks louder than words almost all the time.

I looked at Payal, "Did you ever ask your aunt if she used them as instructed and followed up with her dermatologist on time? Did she take care of her health, particularly her lifestyle? Most important of all, did she ever think of how she handled her emotions?" Everyone looked up at me with a stumped expression.

"As far as I know, she obsessed over her creams. She used to carry them to our vacations as well. And if she forgot them at home, she raised such a ruckus that one of us had to go and buy the entire pharmacy for her," joked Mira.

"Yeah, but did she take care of her health?"

"How do you mean?" asked Payal.

"Did she watch what she ate, when she slept, and her physical activity?" I asked.

"Pradnya, she was her aunt. How many women of your aunt's generation do you know of who do pilates?" laughed Raghav and everyone else with him.

"We know that health and diseases are related, but to say that your skin is affected by an unhealthy routine is a stretch don't you think?" asked Varun. "I mean yes, statistics all point to a lack of exercise leading to heart attacks." The engineer in him harped on this information with pride.

"Health does have a direct correlation to skin diseases" I emphasized. "More so your emotional health or stress as we all know it, can play a very important role in adding to the disease process," I asserted.

"But my aunt wasn't unhappy. Sure, she must have seen her share of bad days, but to say that she was distressed or depressed is like making a mountain out of a molehill. Stress is so common these days. It's normal to have a small amount of stress," affirmed Payal with an unfaltering conviction.

"No amount of stress is normal," I argued.

"Are you telling me that even my sister's acne can be due to emotional stress?" asked Varun laughing loud.

"Yes," I said with patience putting on my dermatologist cap. "Not only that, but you age faster with emotional stress."

"And the cosmetologist speaks," said Raghav with arrogance before I could finish my sentence.

"Which means at age forty, Nihar is going to look like a twenty-year-old because he is living the 'organic' life! And we all will look like sixty years!" said Mira laughing. Nihar raised his glass and gulped down his beer with a smile.

Beads of Swarovski crystals had now started to make an appearance around my hairline as well. The air that filled with the waft of focaccia felt repulsive. I felt a slight flush of embarrassment appear on my cheeks, and lo behold Raghav wasn't helping.

I finally looked at Raghav. "If only your heart could accept that I too am from your fraternity and that I may have a valid point to make, you'd shut the f...ront door!"

Raghav pinched my cheeks and laughed pompously at his success of riling me up. "Come on Pradnya, don't take it so personally." I could sense his patronizing tone.

"Hey guys, chill!" spoke Nihar. "Varun, you dismissed a hard known fact brother. Happy people are healthy people inside out man. Having said that, if my farming and my activities are making me happy and stress-free, then yes, I am going to be living longer. Although I already look like I am a twenty-year-old hunk don't you think?!" He stood up showing off his non – existent paunch.

I looked at everyone smiling and bobbing their heads in affirmation except Mira. "What are you thinking about Mira?" I asked.

"Oh nothing," she said trying to dismiss the question. Everyone went silent. But I wasn't convinced, "Come on, is everything okay?"

There was silence in the group with all eyes on the curly-haired woman. "What you said earlier, about emotions, is it true?" she asked with hesitance.

"Yes. It very much is Mira." I answered. I could hear Varun and Raghav shifting with awkwardness in their seats.

"Can balding be a sign of stress?" She asked.

"Yes!" I said with confidence.

"In that case, the whole world would be bald… Everyone goes through emotional ups and downs," joked Varun breaking the thread of talk. Everyone laughed as expected.

But I wasn't going to give up so soon. My explanation was ready. "Yes, but different emotions can lead to different diseases in different people. Everyone is unique."

"The happier you are, the healthier you are," cheered Nihar, "and that's what I live by."

"Only if being happy was so simple!" said Raghav. "Pray tell us how to be happy?" he asked me straight up with his hands folded in a Namaste.

"You can meditate, exercise, and pursue things that…"

'In an utopian world," Said Varun.

"And even if had a great lifestyle, people still fall sick. My friend who ran marathons underwent an angioplasty at age thirty-five!" said Payal.

The Crazy Five were going crazy. Their thoughts splattering all over the place. "Agreed. But aside from physical health, emotional health is important as well!" No one seemed interested in this statement of mine. It was as if I was killing their party mood. But the doctor in me was being relentless. "Did you know that your emotions are a result of your thoughts, and these thoughts lead to emotions and that causes diseases? It is a vicious cycle, one that cannot get identified and is harmful."

"Then how do you change your thoughts?" asked Mira.

Finally, someone posed the right question. "With one single formula!" I said. I reached into my purse to take out my pen and paper. I laid it across the table and as I was about to write Varun spoke, "Come on Pradnya, a single formula? You sound like those marketers trying to sell a sensation rather than the truth."

"But there is!" I continued in frustration. "It is called the A+B= C formula!"

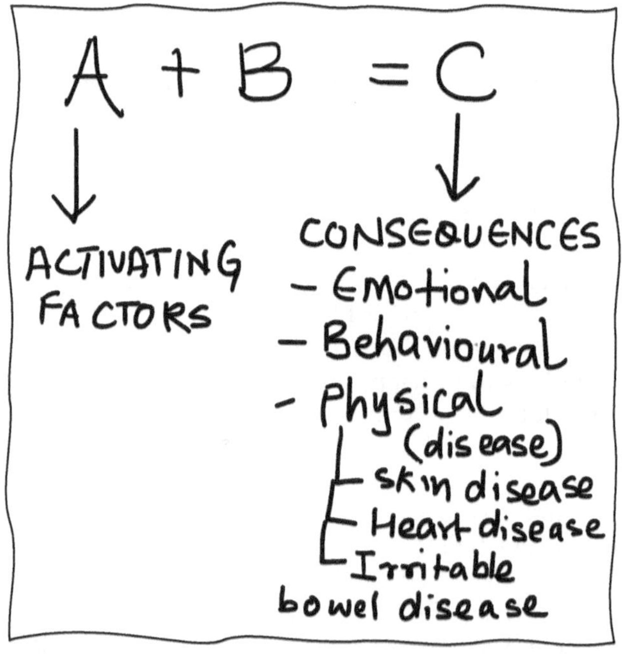

Figure 5.1- A single formula of Rational Emotive Behaviour Therapy (REBT)

Everyone looked at me with suspicion. "Yes, it is that simple. A stands for Activating factors. C for Consequences that are either emotional, behavioural, or even physical, as in diseases in various organs like the skin, heart, lung, etc. Your Activating factors or triggers could be anything from people you don't like, situations that make you uncomfortable, your actions like not finishing a deadline at work, or your negative thoughts about your skin disease or hair problems. Mira, your question on hair, why did you ask that?" I turned to her for an answer.

"I have severe hair fall…!" she seemed worried than ever before.

"Bingo! Your A, activating factor, was your falling hair. Anything else that stresses you out?"

"Gosh, the children just don't listen…" she added.

"Okay, so your Activating factors are multiple, your children not listening and your hair fall. And what would your C, emotional consequence, or simply put – your emotion be whenever you looked at your hair fall on the floor or when you children disobeyed you?"

"I get anxious and angry!" She touched her curly hair as she spoke.

I continued to play my role, "According to you- your hair fall (A) led to your anxiety (C) and your children not listening to you (A) led to your anger (C)?" She nodded in affirmation. "But look at the formula- It's not A= C." Everyone peered once more. The formula read A+B=C. It was only when the B was added to the A, is when you got the C *(Fig 5.2)*.

"What is B?" asked Raghav.

"B is your Belief system. These are your thoughts about the activating factor. A perspective or a viewpoint- I might add- towards how you look at the activating factor. In Mira's case, some belief about her hair is leading to anxiety. We need to find out that B or belief of hers and change it. Only then will she be able to analyse her anxiety and get better results with treatment."

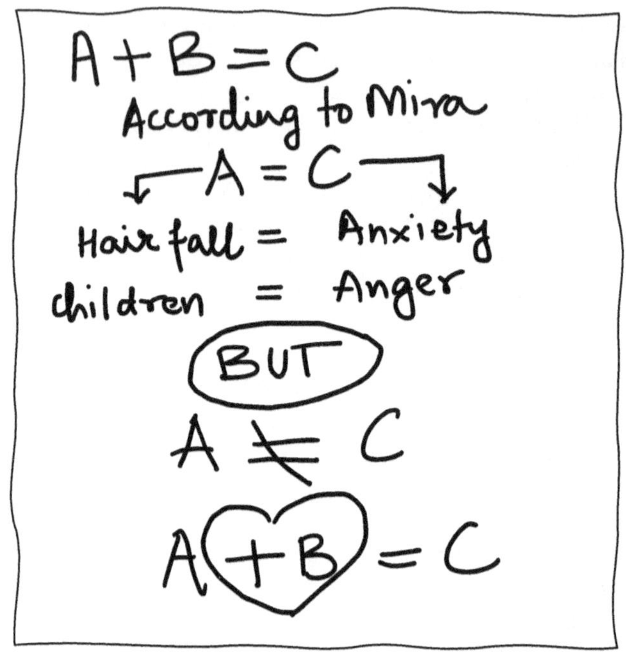

Figure 5.2- Activating factors (A's) do not cause Consequences (C's). B is your Belief system.

"Are you saying, that her hair fall is psychological?" blurted Varun. The word psychological is still a taboo in most societies and so it was in the Crazy Five as well. "Are you saying she is a cuckoo? Or are you saying that dermatologists are not the right doctors to go for hair fall? Because as per this formula, a hair fall patient needs to go to a psychiatrist and not come to you!"

"Look here," I said and continued to draw.

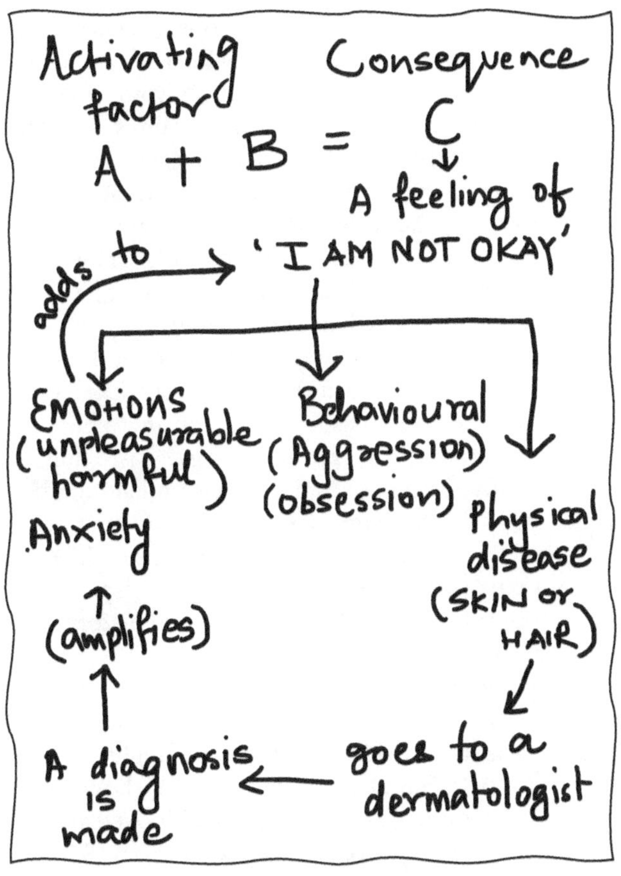

Figure 5.3- The vicious Thought- Disease loop. Activating factors (A's) makes you believe that something is wrong with you. This further leads to emotional consequences.

"There is a Thought-Disease loop that is running in the mind. And as I said, every time you get a thought that is harmful, you start experiencing consequences either in the form of unpleasurable emotions, in behaviour, or physically in the form of a skin disease. Your A's create a 'I am not okay' feeling in you. If this feeling of something is wrong leads to emotional and behavioral consequences, then yes, you would probably end up at a psychiatrist's doorstep. But if you had physical manifestations in your skin, then a dermatologist would be your choice. Mira's hair fall is a physical manifestation of her A's or triggers. And this hair fall is further worsening her emotional well-being or C. So in order to help Mira, we need to treat her hair fall and alongside also help her deal with other triggers like how to deal with her children when they disobey. Get it?" I looked around to see if anyone had understood.

The Crazy Five just stared at the paper and then at me turn by turn. I put my pen down and wiped the sweat off my forehead with the tissue that lay on the table. For the second time today, my Circuit of Logic was being raided. The Crazy Five being Loki's flock and terminating Thor (my Circuit of Logic), that under conducive circumstances, could have given Varun a logical response. The logical thinking part of my brain was fried to a crisp. Against all odds, I started to speak. "Do you know the story of a boy who heard God's voice?"

Everyone looked flabbergasted. Raghav touched his palm to my forehead to check if I had gone viral! I stood my ground against the backdrop of intense laughter, "This is a story by Gopal Gaur Das narrated on a TV show that I saw. It seems relevant to our conversation." I looked at everyone with calm. "There was once a boy who was walking home. One fine day, he heard a voice say to him, *'Push the mountain that you see in front of you.'* The boy, curious to know where the voice came around, searched all around the road to see who had said the words. He searched high and low, east and west but to no avail. *'This must be God,'* he told himself. *'God wants me to push the mountain.'* Every day he went up to the mountain and tried to push it. Not a day did he miss. A year went by, and the mountain had not moved even a millimeter. He looked up at the bright blue sky and yelled in agony. Disappointed in himself, he gave up and went home. *'Why did you ask me to do something that wasn't going to happen*

God?' he asked through the pain of failure that he was feeling. *'My dear boy,'* said the voice, *'I asked you to push the mountain, not move it. Now, are you ready to listen to me?'*

We often hear and do not listen. I see this everywhere. The Crazy Five had fallen prey to this habit. Everyone was looking at me as if I were an alien from Mars trying to teach them a new language. I had lost the battle even before it had begun.

To my pleasant surprise Raghav was quiet. "Don't bother to explain," he muttered into my ear with an empathetic tone. I looked at him trying to study his intention. Empathy was not his strong point. He smiled and continued, "No one will understand Pradnya. Everyone wants a quick fix solution these days. Creams in your case and surgery in my case. There is a simple rule that many of us surgeons follow: Get in and get out. Don't dwell and try to change any belief process or system or whatever it is that you want to name it. Because the patient won't change, and you end up getting hurt. That is what keeps us, at least me, sane in this insane sea of heart attacks."

A shiver ran down my spine. "Yes, but that doesn't mean you give up on them." I still tried to debate in my state of mental exhaustion.

"You don't give up on them, you still treat them. What I am saying is – don't try to change them," said Raghav.

"I know you can't change people unless they want to change themselves… But…"

He only smiled raising his glass and took a sip. That was the end of that conversation. That was the end of all conversations I was going to make at the table that night.

The word *change* echoed in my ears. Was I supposed to pick up my glass and accept the fact that people did not change? Was I supposed to accept that people like Mr S would continue to get mediocre results with creams? I glanced at everyone one more time. As much as I was mentally exhausted, I picked up my glass and made a vow to myself: 'It didn't matter whether people changed or not. What mattered was what I did to help them understand, that change was, in fact, the only way to their redemption.'

I had not heard but listened to what everyone had to say today. And I would patiently wait till they were ready to listen to me.

My Circuit of Logic was starting to reboot. And in that moment, little did I know that Payal, the fittest and most logical headed, would be the first of the Crazy Five to want to hear me out.

Here is Payal's acne story.

Shall we begin to change?

6

Payal's Acne Story
A+B= C is finally heard

I do not fix problems. I fix my thinking. Then problems fix
themselves.
~ Louise L Hay

It is heart-breaking when a beauty with the most breath-taking auburn eyes, shoulder-length straight brown hair, firm shoulders from years of exercising, and aerial yoga peering at you with big drops of tears falling off her cheeks.

Her face was covered with acne in various forms: comedones, red inflamed acne, and some pigmented marks. Crying had made her cheeks and the acne go a shade redder.

I could feel her frustration, not only as a friend but also as a dermatologist. For a person like her, to have healthy glowing skin for most of her life and then to get a burst of large red inflamed acne covering her face is worrying. It defies the logical reason that a fit and healthy person cannot get health issues. I could sense this logic getting questioned in her mind as she sniffed and sobbed. Add to this, the social embarrassment that comes from acne, was even more tormenting especially when you are about to get married in the next six months.

She dumped at least a dozen tubes and bottles combined, on my table in my consulting room. She was carrying a dozen prescriptions from her doctors in Singapore. I read them with patience. She had used a lot of products from Tretinoin cream, Glycolic acid cream, Benzoyl Peroxide gel, Clindamycin gel, and facewashes. Under the guise of organic and plant-based, all that grew in the Amazon forest seemed to be present in one of the

41

facewash she was using.

I saw her peering into the mirror that is always placed on my consulting table. She had picked up the mirror and was touching her acne, in the hope that somehow, they would magically go away.

"When did this start?" I asked breaking her chain of thought.

"Six months ago." She kept touching her acne.

I looked at her papers again. A list of treatments filled the papers. She had undergone chemical peels, laser treatments, red light therapy, photo-facials, over the past 6 months with little or no response. "Any medical issues like thyroid or any other illness that might have triggered this acne?" This question of mine made no sense to her.

"No! I had all my tests done and nothing showed up!" she yelled.

Here was this smart, intelligent, successful career woman, who got up every morning by 6 am, exercised to keep her body healthy, knew how to eat and when to eat, and slept off at 10 pm. It was this discipline that had brought her all her achievements. Yet, Payal's case was not intriguing to me. I see many patients who are healthy and conscious of their lifestyle and still end up with various skin diseases. And I knew in which direction my questioning needed to go.

Me asking her if her lifestyle was on track was like challenging a bull head-on. I knew she had it all sorted. But I also knew the one important fact that she had not considered her marriage that was happening in six months. Her A- Activating factor- was staring her right in the eye and she wasn't paying any heed to it.

Marriage is a life-changing event in a young career woman's life, albeit a happy one, it is life-changing. I helped myself to a pen and paper.

"More creams?" she yelped like a small puppy. The silence that followed filled with her sniffles.

I jotted down A + B = C. "Remember this formula?"

$$A + B = C$$

Fig. 6.1 The Single Formula of REBT

She peered at it through misty eyes, "no."

"Are you facing any stress off late?" I asked.

"Yes, with work, but that's just the routine stress I have," she responded fidgeting with her wristwatch. If you remember correctly- this is the same Payal, from Crazy Five, who was convinced that 'it was normal to have Stress'.

"Anything different from the usual stress?"

She moved her head from side to side and stared at me. I had come to a dead point.

For all those people, who have led life believing that stress is a regular phenomenon, they all are living- on- the- edge daredevils. These are the people who live off the adrenaline rush that comes along with stress; Adrenaline junkies as they are often known. The morning kick of the hormone drives them through the day, and they consider it a normal phenomenon. This makes them tough but doesn't make them resilient. Being tough is like being the Berlin wall- hard on the outside and emotionally repressed inside. Resilience is like a regular picket fence and does the job of keeping out intruders (illogical/harmful thoughts). When we get tough, we have gotten used to the regular irritating triggers like jobs, bosses, family, etc. But when we get resilient, we have not only gotten used to these triggers but are not affected by them as much. They continue to exist in harmony around us despite their irritating nature. Honestly, stress as a word has been abused. Because not everything that you see as a challenge, or a trigger is a stress. We as people have started to believe that anything that puts you out of your comfort zone is stress. Stress, as we know it, does put you in discomfort, but if your response to the stress was appropriate then that would make you resilient and help you deal with it in a better way. And such stress that generates an appropriate behaviour from you is called Eustress. If a stress generated an underreaction or an overreaction from you, then that would be called Distress. For example, if your mother kept saying hurtful things and you ignored her instead of respectfully telling her to back off- that would be an underreaction to the stress. If you ran after her with a shovel in your hand, that would be an overreaction! This distress (underreaction or overreaction) is what we have started labelling as stress. Eustress helps you do better and progress in your endeavours. It's like a challenge thrown at you- that you deal with- in a proper time, with the proper use of your resources, and with the emotional capacity that you have in you at that stage of your life. Distress is the bad boy, the normal stress as we call it these days, that makes you an addict to adrenaline as was the case with Payal. Her distress was now her stress and she had become ignorant to the fact that she needed to do something about it. Deeming any amount of distress (like the maid not coming for work, the boss yelling, losing a loved one, or a catastrophe like the Tsunami) as normal is like saying I have normal diabetes. How many people have you come across who say, '*Arre yaar, normal diabetes hai*'?

This next question that I asked is my favorite question, which usually stumps the adrenaline junkie. "How would you define *your* stress?" Like most of my patients who don't have convincing answers neither did Payal. She looked at me with a blank expression. I continued, "Would you agree that stress is omnipresent?"

"Yes." She agreed. "Does stress, any amount of it, make you feel good at all?"

"No."

"What does it make you feel?"

"Bad!"

"How many times in a day are you not feeling good?"
She thought for a moment. "Many."
"Can you recollect how many? I'll give you ten seconds."
She looked irritated. "I need more than ten seconds to know how many times I don't feel good Pradnya."
I smiled, "And because you are feeling not-so-good many times a day, your hormones are having a field day. There is your answer for why nothing is working- creams or treatments. The moment you feel stress because of a negative thought, it starts a cascade of events…" I started to draw a flow chart with my pen.

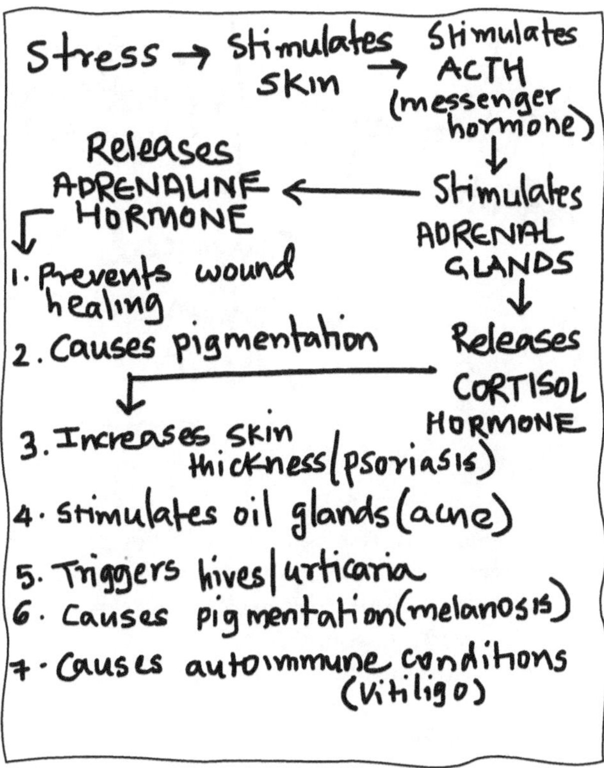

Fig. 6.2- Stress stimulates hormones that cause various skin diseases

These Hormones are a sort of drug cartel- With Cortisol and Adrenaline being the El Chapo and El Mayo, and they are the reason for all the magic, rather dark magic? Adrenalin also had effects on the bacteria that cause acne and this can cause excess production of sebum by the oil gland, which causes acne.

I pointed her to the formula A+ B =C that I had written.

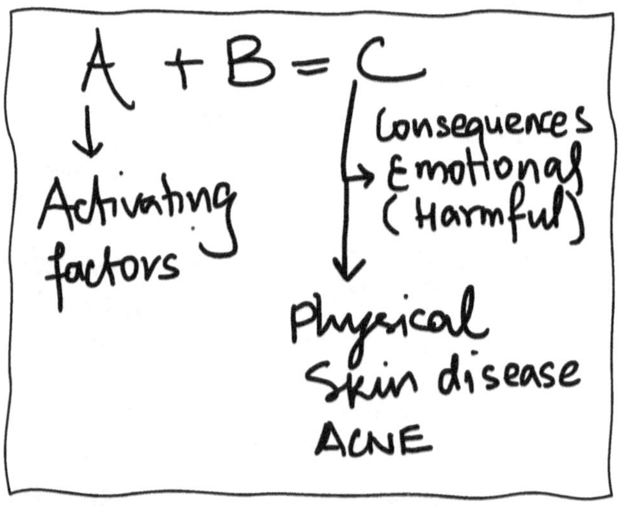

Fig. 6.3

I repeated how A stood for activating factor, B for Belief system, and C for emotional consequences. "Let's agree," I said, "that your stress makes you feel not so good." She nodded in affirmation.

"If A= Activating factor (unpleasurable event big or small). Can you tell me what is your A?" I asked.

She thought for a while and said her A was her marriage that was due in 6 months and there were many things left to do.

Activation factors aren't very hard to identify. As I

mentioned, these are the ugly heads that keep showing up around you day in and day out. And they need not be catastrophic like the Tsunami either. Your A could be your boss and his nagging, or the fact that your maid hasn't shown up for work for the third time in a month, or your exam results, or a big promotion that is due. Because you are surrounded by these factors, and because you cannot change them in real time and immediately, you incorporate them into your life and start considering them as 'routine,' or '*roj ka kat kat*'*. These daily irritating events are your activating factors and are causing micro-spurts of adrenaline into the system. They can be as mundane as the above-mentioned examples, or Tsunami- like, or a death of a loved one, the fall of a building, or a marriage coming up as in Payal's case. Most people would consider marriage a happy and joyful event, something that everyone in the family, young or old, rich or poor, looks forward to. But behind the mirth of marriage, lies the mountain of logistical responsibilities. The venue finalization, the happiness of the in-laws, the shopping, etc, and the list is endless. How many marriages have you been to where you have not noticed the stress on the faces of the mother and father of the bride and groom? It's like a now-or-never situation, more like a do-or-die situation, where the merriment of marriage falls aside and marriage becomes another task that needs to be carried out flawlessly.

I moved on to the C part of the equation. C equals the emotional consequence or turmoil that the Activating factors incite. Emotional consequences translate to the emotions incited in you, when you feel stressed out. It is always the negative emotions that are detrimental. And they can ride on your back as silent as the ghost Vetal who rode on King Vikram's back. They are hovering around you, unbeknownst to you. I asked her to name all the negative emotions she felt when her triggering factor was active.

There was pin-drop silence for a while. "Fear, anger, sadness, anxiety…" she said quietly after she had given it

47

some thought.

"Which emotion affects you more? Which emotion are you operating on?"

She pondered for a while and answered, "fear".

"Have you noticed the equation?" I asked her coyly. She glanced at it again. "Yes, it says A+ B= C."

I smiled, "We covered A and we covered C, what do you think is B?"

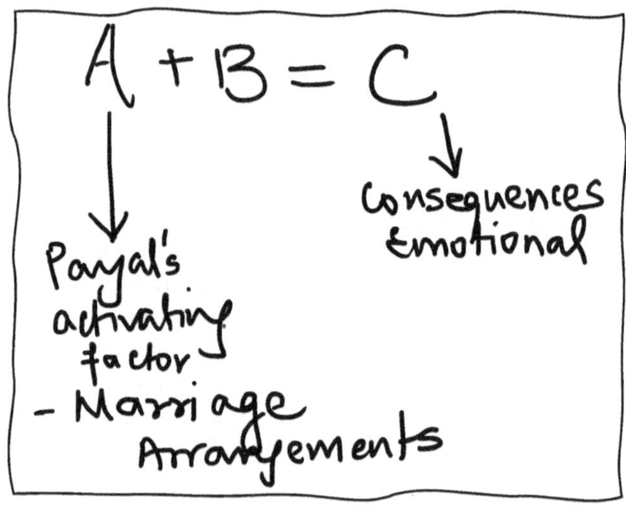

Fig. 6.4- She listed her Activating factor (A)

This is the first time she smiled as well. "I have no clue!" she said, sitting up straight with an eagerness to know the answer.

"B is your belief system," I uttered.

This is the hardcore truth- *Your* irrational belief systems cause your emotional or physical consequences. It's never your A that causes them. It is when your ideas or thoughts or perception get added to the activating factor is when you get consequences. Once you realise this B, it changes the way you face the outer world. It also changes your perception of your inner world. Payal could see that A was not equal to C. Your activating factors don't cause emotional consequences as seen in *fig 5.2*. It is only when your belief systems were added to your activating factors did you get those unhealthy emotions. The Eureka moment shined in her eyes. The magic of thinking had already begun. I am not saying we don't think. Rather we overthink, and in a manner that does not help us. We think without being aware of our thoughts and amplify the A's and the C's. To explain in simple terms, we tend to make a mountain out of a mole hill. Look at the figure below:

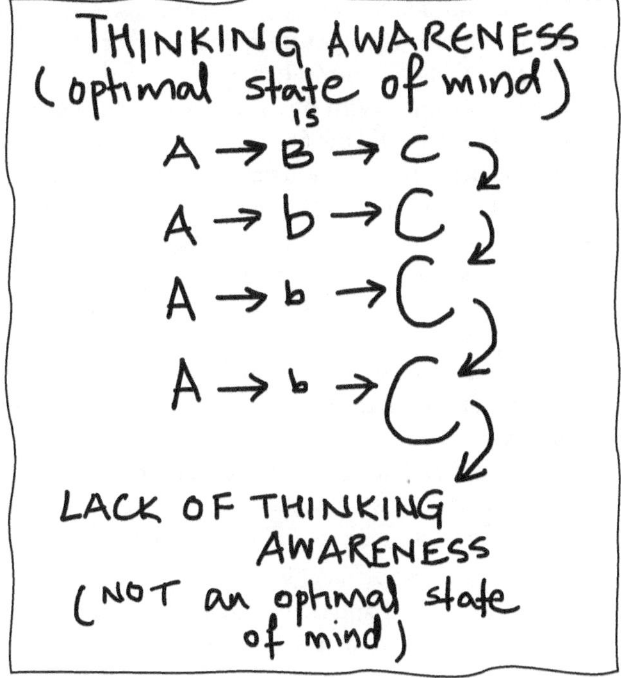

Fig. 6.5- We magnify our A's (irritating events) and C's (harmful emotions) and forget that an irrational B exists

When we are aware of our thinking, we tend to analyze not only the irritating trigger and the emotional consequence, but also the irrational belief that resulted in the consequence. But as 'thinking awareness' goes down and is replaced by untamed thinking, we see how we lose the balance in our analysis by forgetting to think about the belief. Yes, we forget that there is a factor called the belief system that leads to all our discomfort. And Payal had also forgotten it. Of the three - A, B, and C, the only thing she could change, rather she had the complete power to change was her belief system. 'What could you change at any given moment in time, especially *now*, as we speak?" I asked with excitement.

As she continued to gaze at me I asked asked her, "How would you apply this to yourself, that is your life today?" She stared at the paper. Her eyes moved across the handwritten formula. With furrowed brows, she asked with hesitance, "I understand my fear around my marriage. What could be my belief be? I have always wanted to get married."

"Can you think of any statement with a *must* or *should* in it?" I asked softening my tone. "What will happen if the marriage arrangements aren't according to your vision?"

"They *must* be! I will work hard to see to it that they are!" she answered without a pause. Her *must* had started to show its ugly head and she was still oblivious to it.

"Why must your marriage arrangements be flawless? So what if someone complains?" I asked.

"That *should not* happen. I will not let it happen."

"Why?" I smiled as I asked.

Streams of tears started rolling down her eyes, "That means — I would have failed!"

I got up to hug her and asked. "Are you marrying so that you pass a test called marriage... Or because you are in love?"

The sobbing stopped and her eyes fixed on mine. The moment of realization had dawned in them.

That she *must* arrange for her wedding in a manner befitting her and her fiancé's status plagued her. That she *must* look pretty on her wedding day, and she *should* be impeccably adorned with jaw-dropping jewellery, were some of her irrational beliefs that were creating fear. Again, there is nothing wrong in having a big lavish wedding or the best jewellery in the world on you. But what hurts is forgetting why you are doing what you are doing? Is it to show the world or to be happy? Is to prove a point or be content that you did the best you could? As much as it was okay for Payal to have these expectations, she was being equally unfair to herself because all these expectations had to be fulfilled without failure. That's like being the God of the God of the Gods – if such a thing existed, because even the Gods that I know of have failed at some point only to rise stronger and better. Failure doesn't make you any less of a person, it teaches you to be more of a person that you already are, but in a different way.

Fig. 6.6- Payal enlisted her Must's and Should's

The light in her eyes had returned. She took the piece of paper which we had used as a worksheet and studied it again. In the tone of a wise sage she asked," How do we change ourselves?"

I knew at that precise moment that she would heal her acne.

As a dermatologist, I see so many patients being unkind to themselves. As a human species, the one thing we are capable of and which makes us distinct from other species, is kindness. We know kindness even before anyone has taught us what it meant. If we are kind to strangers on a bus, then why are we not kind to ourselves? Why are we so critical of ourselves? Why do we put ourselves on so high a pedestal, that we have to sacrifice our health, in Payal's case-her skin health, to achieve it? Because of the influence of the world; rather an influence that we allow the world to create in us. Because we think we need to look, dress, behave or do things in a certain way without which we wouldn't be good enough for the world. We want validation because we as humans are always seeking a sense of belong. And to gratify this sense of belongingness, we are seeking validation from others.

Think about it. How many Payal's are there who realize that marriage is between two hearts and not a show for the world? Not a lot. It is not about right or wrong. You could have the world's most expensive wedding and yet be unhappy or it could be a private matter between two sets of families and still feel be a joyful event. You could even elope and it would be the most happiness you experienced. Marriage, at least as I have seen it, becomes a symbol of power, success, money, and satisfaction. But along with this, it becomes a strenuous activity that drains the most important resource we have- our precious emotional energy. As I said, it is not about right or wrong. It is always about how you handle the biggest truth there is- of knowing that you are but a human and you are fallible. And that your beliefs need not be someone else's, that despite trying you could fail, and even if you did fail, the world would think little of you – only if you thought little of yourself. This power of belief about yourself always rested in you. Only that, you weren't told that it did. All you had to do was change yourself, rather, change the way you looked at yourself.

I treated Payal with the usual line of medicines. And our process of change began. Change in not only her skin but also her beliefs.

But are these beliefs the same for all people, or did they differ from person to person? I had never imagined that Varun would end up asking me these questions. Varun's story was completely different from Payal's. Shall we continue to change?

Varun's Vitiligo Story
Belief can be a Bitch

Man is made by his beliefs. As he believes, so he is.
~Anon

…he confuses his self, his total personality with his performances, and he automatically evaluates and rates the former along with the latter. Consequently, he very frequently ends up by damning himself and other people (that is, denigrating his and their intrinsic value) rather than merely appraising the efficacy or desirability of his or their performances (his and their extrinsic value).
~ Dr Albert Ellis

"Hi, Tycoon!" I exclaimed.

A very mellowed hello was what I heard. Like someone or something had sucked the life out of him. I could feel the phone go cold. Imagine such as meek reply coming from a guy whose hello on the phone my mother could hear sitting in the other room.

"What happened?" I asked mortified thinking someone had died.

"Nothing. How are you?" He retorted.

"Couldn't be better!" I could hear the cars and his kids squealing in the background. The only sign that he was on the line was that the occasional rustle of paper.

"Are you counting your monies?!"

"No…" his voice trailed off in the far distance.

Varun had been a very successful entrepreneur so far. He was an engineer and after his MBA from the Indian Institute of Management in Calcutta, the prophecy that he would be a young success in no time turned out to be true.

I remember the happiness on his face when he first announced his startup. This baby of his grew fast and enough, to be acquitted by the biggest shark in the market. Any one of us would have enjoyed the rest of our lives on the amount made, but Varun wasn't any one of us. He was the go-getter, and he went and started another company. We all looked at him with awe. By now he had a wife, and one kid was on the way. But that wasn't going to deter him. Au contraire, it turned out to be the most important driving factor there is. By the time his second company was also a big success, was acquired as well, his second child Arya was born.

"He could go buy a five storied bungalow with a yard so big that he could land his helicopter and fly off to his island and back!" Nihar had once joked when we all met at the last reunion.

But we were all wrong. There was a third company now growing as fast as the last one. He was working as long as twelve to fourteen hours a day. Coming home, he managed to play with his kids who craved for his attention, talk to his wife about her day, and enquire how his parents were. I always wondered how he managed to keep everyone around him happy. When, after a day of intense work, all you want to do is to freshen up and sit with a single malt in your hands, this man was living up to everyone's expectations. I used to be in awe of Varun for managing it so well. Never did I hear him complain or see his wife unhappy. As I said, this sweet guy, the charmer, was all that everyone saw.

"Come on Varun!" I jibed. "You can tell me what's wrong."

"Everything!" he yelled back. The kids stopped playing in the background. Only the cars were audible and his wife from the far end. "Why are you yelling again? The kids get sacred!" she retorted. This is when I knew something had gone wrong. I knew his wife, and there was no way that she could be so curt. And none of us had ever encountered the two fight. Before I could come up with something to say,

Varun spoke, "Let's meet?" He asked echoing my thoughts, "Have some news to share."

The whole ride to Lonavala, where we had decided to meet, I could only think of what 'news' was he to give. Because there was always something huge up his sleeve. Either he was announcing his company or the arrival of his babies or a trip to Europe and whatnot. And being the charmer he was, we all went with his boastful bantering. But as good a charmer he was, he was also a kind man with a big heart. He often donated to various charities and he funded Nihar out in his early days of farming. Not to forget the love and dedication he showed to his family was laudable. How could anyone of us not love this kind, compassionate, ever cheerful, charming man?

I reached the resort early and settled down in their poolside restaurant. The rains had begun. The hillside view of Lonavala reflected various shades of green. My favourite flower the *chafa** was in bloom and its fragrance spread a silent cheer. A tiny bird had planted itself on the chair in front of me, without fear. It sat there, looking at the table and hoping to steal a small crumble of bread off of it. Its vibrant yellow color stood out as bright as the sun against a backdrop of the green. As I was about to extend my hand towards the bird, I heard someone come up and stand behind me.

"Hi, beautiful!" Varun said. I got up and hugged him. He was a huge teddy bear, smart, tall, with a cute boyish face who towered over you. As we sat on our seats, I could see a hint of a double chin and some added weight around his waist, with a few grey hairs and dark circles. As I searched his face, I went stone cold. I saw at the corner of his lips a tiny hint of a white patch. Panic stricken, I then searched other exposed areas and saw hints of pure white on his fingertips. He had developed vitiligo- a kind of leucoderma. I was so engrossed in my search for patches that even the waiter who was waiting on the next table was watching me with intrigue.

57

"Yes… This!" He lifted his hands and showed the white patches to me. "It has been four months," he said. "At first I thought I got hurt after which I got a patch on the finger. But then over the next month, new ones started appearing and this is how far it has progressed."

"Why didn't you call me?" I asked reaching out my hand to touch the patches on his fingertips.

"I visited a dermatologist in Pune," he said as a matter of fact.

"And has the treatment helped?" I asked with a hint of annoyance because he hadn't reached out to me first.

"It has to some extent. But the oral steroids are making me bloat." He made a balloon face to make me laugh. I was still examining his patches oblivious to his antics. "All the reports are normal. And no one in my family has had it. I have no idea why this would happen." He said shrugging his shoulders.

I finally looked up and smiled at this statement, "Genes don't matter anymore Varun. The age-old solid concept that genes cause disease is being challenged by the new age concept that genes do not matter as much. What matters is Epigenetics. The detrimental influence of your physical environment and your emotional turmoil on your genes decides if you get a disease- skin or otherwise. You may or may not have inherited the genes."

He was sitting up straight with his hands rested on the table, fingers entwined. The cool breeze made his hair cover a part of his face, softening the hint of worry line that was appearing on his forehead. "Vitiligo is an autoimmune disease," I continued, "where your own (auto), defense cells (immune cells) start acting against your body. They attack your color-producing cells and kill them. If the person has been unhealthy with a bad lifestyle, then chances are the Vitiligo could progress faster and stay longer."

Varun had always neglected his health. Behind his need to start his own companies, nurture them, and grow them, he could never find time for exercise. His sleep patterns were irregular. Because he never put on weight, he assumed he was fit enough. He seemed older than he was. Add to that the mental stress that one faces while starting something new is bound to trigger all sorts of genetic diseases, whether you had the gene or not. Varun was a perfect example of how epigenetics played a role in manifesting the autoimmune disease for him. If you check the flow chart in Payal's story *(Fig 6.2)*, you will notice how microbursts of adrenaline and cortisol, both can trigger the immune system introducing hostile defense cells. As I explained to him the concept of the neurocutaneous immune system, also called the NCIS, his eyes started to show some hope. The nagging question of why he got the disease when no one in the family had it was finally getting answered. "So, it's the stress that is causing this?" He asked.

"Yes, and the bad sleeping plus eating habits are adding to the oxidative damages that are happening in your skin. They are killing off the melanocytes or the color-producing cells in your skin." I added.

"You mean, I don't look like a twenty-five-year-old?" he joked, making us both laugh. I could see that the charmer was coming round.

"But stress is every where isn't it? How do you not get affected by it?"

His question was genuine. Payal's concept of stress was that it was 'normal' to have it and Varun considered it omnipresent. And as Payal had been ignorant of her distress, Varun was overreacting to his. That is where I took out the pen and paper from my bag, my eternal weapon of mass information, to write down the formula A+B=C. And as I had explained to Payal the formula, I started telling Varun about the Activating factors (A) and how they led to emotional consequences (C). As we continued to debate and discuss, he realised that one of his A's was his children. When he came home from work and his children climbed all over him for attention, it led to a feeling of irritation. One would think of this thought as heartless. But as heartless as sounds, it isn't. Despite the love for his children, he felt annoyed because he would come home tired from the day's work, too tired to entertain his children. But this very same love was the reason he would give in to his children's demands and end up playing with them, when all he would want is some *me* time.

But remember the formula?

A is not equal to C. Triggers did not cause emotional consequences or physical consequences in the form of skin disease. It was only after he added his irrational belief systems to the activating factors that he ended up with unpleasurable emotions. We tried to go deeper into Varun's thoughts. What could his irrational belief systems be? As a father, he had grown to believe that he *must* under any circumstance, at any point of time, and all the time, be able to give attention to his children no matter how tired he was. It was a primary duty, one that could not be compromised on at any cost. Because he was never fully around, the guilt prevented him from saying no to his children. As much as it is a need to be dutiful, the *demand* to be dutiful- always, whenever, however- ends up being frustrating and irritating to the person carrying out the duty, be it for a father, mother, sister, etc or any other role that is being played. The mere act of duty becomes important and not the way it is being performed. For example, Varun spent time with his kids as a duty despite being tired. Neither did Varun enjoy nor his kids. The demand in his head to perform a duty as was asked of him, whenever and wherever, ended up with him being spending quantitative time and not qualitative time with his children.

There was another point of discussion that came up about how he felt about all his startups. His relationship with his startups was very intricate. These companies were not only something that he started, but he had come to associate them with his image- his self-worth. He thought that he had gotten respect and fame because of his companies. Otherwise, no one would know he even existed. He convinced himself that it was due to his achievements that people had started to take note of him and not because of the person he was. And he considered any negative event or word about his startups as a personal setback. That hurt his ego and decreases his self-worth. His irrational belief was: To maintain this impeccable identity of his, he needed to ensure his companies were a symbol of utmost perfection. His belief system was that he *must* flawlessly run his companies if he has to preserve this untarnished image of himself in front of the world. His self-worth rested on how well the companies run, not in the confidence that he was good enough in the first place for starting the companies at all.

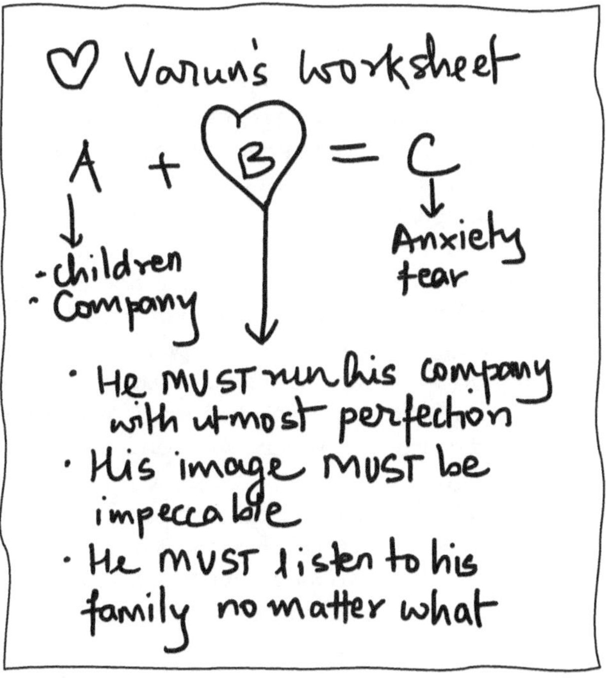

Fig. 7.1- Varun's worksheet

Such irrational beliefs can be very tiring to a person who has been working non-stop for the past ten years. The burnout rate is faster in such cases and for Varun, the white patches on his fingertips against the light brown skin was proof enough.

The engineer in him asked me a question, "Aren't belief systems important? Aren't they akin to morality? As a father isn't it a moral duty to give time to my children when they want?"

Belief systems are very subjective systems. And as I said, there are irrational and rational ones too. Beliefs are personal thoughts that the person carries about people, places, things, politics, environment, the dog next door, Harry Potter… and the list is endless. These are thoughts that the person has developed over the years of living life. Belief systems can be formed or they can be borrowed. A belief is born through three steps- experience, acquisition and perpetuation. And belief systems are born when you are born! Literally! As a child, I listen to my parent's experience of how beer tastes bad and since I am not able to taste alcohol at that age, I *acquire* it as my experience and *perpetuate* the thought that beer is indeed yucky to taste till I am all of eighteen years of age, and have had the first glass of the golden blissful beer myself, only to find out that beer isn't so bad in taste after all! From the inception of my belief of beer being yucky in taste to the transformation of my belief that beer is an awesome drink happened over the years through experience, acquisition, and perpetuation of the thought, in a gradual way. At times, some experiences as a child are direct. We experience friendship at that tender age and make our own beliefs of what it is to be a 'best' friend. We acquire this belief as our own and perpetuate the idea of a best friend. And at some point, if we get unlucky, then we experience the betrayal of the best friend and change our beliefs of friendship. And if we are lucky, we continue to live by this belief of the bestie. This experience, acquisition, perpetuation is happening all the time over the years. Even as you read this book, in this very instant, you are going through the same process- either making new beliefs or breaking older ones.

As a child, I remember the controversy when Michael Jackson had decided to change his color. Back then, I was too tiny to understand the racial angle behind it, but for me the curiosity lay in how a person could change all of his skin color. When I started studying dermatology is when I realized that he had developed vitiligo. Because his disease was progressive, he chose to depigment himself rather than re-pigment himself with Trioxsalen or PUVA therapy or oral steroids. Today, as I write this, I wonder what his belief system was that he chose to lose all colour in his skin, become white, and suffer the accusation of being racist, than live with the disease. Maybe he believed that he *must not* have defective skin or he *must* be perfect in his appearance like he was perfect in his music, even if it meant being labelled a racist? This is all just speculation and we may never know what he thought. But he certainly, without an iota of doubt, had his *must's* and s*hould's* in the irrational beliefs he carried about the disease called vitiligo or even about his image and skill. Today, years after Michael Jackson, when I open my Instagram account and scroll, I see beautiful images of a model called Winnie Harlow, who also has vitiligo but chooses not to hide it. I wonder what her beliefs about skin or her image are? I am certain that they are far different from Michael Jackson's, as she flaunts the beautiful color pattern that forms on her skin for everyone to see. Everyone has their belief systems. But they need not always be a moralistic view towards life. My belief that I *must* look to the right and left of the road before I cross helps me prevent an accident. Where is the moralistic attitude in that? It is more of a life-saving attitude, a basic instinct against a biological threat, a rational determined *must* and not an irrational obstinate *must*.

But to answer Varun's question of moralistic beliefs, the answer was simple yet complex. His children deserved his time, giving time to them only because it fit his image of being a good father was unfair to the the kids and him. Under the guise of morality, wouldn't it help more if he had made time for them like he made a time for his work? That way, he would live up to his image of being a father, be much prepared when he got home, and more mentally fresh to spend time with his children. More than the quantity of time, it was about the quality of time he gave his children or his wife or even his parents.

If he made time, say if he decided that every day between 8 pm to 9 pm would be for his children, where he would focus only on giving them attention without taking phone calls, or looking at emails, his children would probably appreciate it better.

A belief system is an ideology or a set of principles that help us to interpret our everyday reality. This could be in the form of religion, political affiliation, philosophy, or spirituality, among many other things. These beliefs are being shaped and influenced by several different factors. Belief systems hold the person and the society as a large in place. I do believe that are great equalizers as well. My belief that I must cross the road after I have looked to the right and left helps me not only to survive but also protects the driver of the car from legal action if we would have run over me. And this belief system works for everyone, no matter age, sex, caste, creed, or nationality. Many such belief systems work for us and are deemed moralistic: I *must not* hurt anyone, I *must* be kind, I *must* not steal, I *must* not lie (at least not all the time). They help us see the good in ourselves and others. But then there are those belief systems that don't work for us anymore. In effect, there are workable belief systems and non- workable belief systems. Workable ones are the ones that benefit us at a certain point of time. The important phrase is 'at a certain point in time'. At some other point, this same belief system might need some rework. If we took Varun's example, his belief system that he *must* give time to his children when *they* wanted it worked in the first three years of fatherhood. Because then, work wasn't so consuming all his time. He had free time and less stress because his first company was already up and thriving when the kids were born. After his second company and his third company, a lot of things changed. He had more people working for him. He had added financial responsibilities towards these people and his company. And his children weren't young anymore, they had grown up into, what I like to call mini-adults, and they wanted more quality time from their father. Only a mere dance and kiss from daddy didn't suffice. They wanted more attention from him and most of all, they understood when he couldn't give them that attention. After ten years, this same belief system, that he *must* give time to his children when they wanted it, had become redundant and non-workable. So, what would make life easier? Changing this redundant belief and making place for newer ones. If the belief system continued, there would be only irritation and the interaction with his kids would be unpleasant.

His second belief was a sort of extension of his first belief; That he *must* be perfect when it came to his company. A perfect company meant he was perfect. He started to correlate the company image with his own. I cannot tell you how many people I have seen suffer because of this one belief system. Varun's counterargument was valid: That it was this perfectionist attitude that had got him to where he was. And I agreed. But now, as we sat at the restaurant in Lonavala when the need for perfection was sucking the joy out of running the project, that belief had to change. This attitude was productive ten years ago when he was younger with lesser responsibilities. But now, he had chosen other responsibilities, which also needed his time and demanded his perfectionist attitude.

"Maybe it was time to let go of a little control," I said. "Rather to start regulating your irrational beliefs. It is high time that you started reflecting on your *mus'ts* that are irrational and *should's* that work for you. Don't you think?"

The bird was back, perching on the empty chair. Looking eagerly at the half-eaten Focaccia bread on the table. And before I could push the plate towards the little thing, Varun had already extended the bread he had in his hand. The little one grabbed at it and flew away.

"Daring little thing wasn't he?" He smiled.

"Yeah daring and cute!" I said.

"Daring as I am and cute like you are Champa Chameli!"

The charmer had started to rise with this funny banter and his name-calling. He was the loveable Teddy Bear indeed. He never stopped making me feel special. Maya Angelou said- *"I've learned that people will forget what you said, people will forget what you did, but people will never forget how you made them feel."*

Varun was a living example of this and looking at how dedicated a father he had grown to be, it always reminded me of Mira. Mira's skills of mothering were extraordinary. She was patient and caring of everyone and like Varun was also a perfect example of how she was loved because of how she made others feel. But as much as this is true, what is the price that we pay to make others feel good? Is there a line that we need to draw? Mira's hair fall was edging her towards realizing that even before anyone else, it mattered how *I* made *me* feel. Mira's hair fall would be a catalyst for changing her into a more loving person than she already was…

Mira's Hair Thinning Story
Don't put people in Temples or Templates

To see with the eyes of another, to hear with the ears of another, to feel with the heart of another. For the time being, this seems to me an admissible definition of what we call social feeling.
~Alfred Adler

I could die for you. But I couldn't and wouldn't live for you.
~Ayn Rand (The Fountainhead)

I must undertake to love myself and respect myself and to respect myself as though my very life depends upon self-love and self-respect.
~Maya Angelou

It was 9 am in the morning. And as a ritual, I had opened the browser on my phone to read an article on hair. Not to my surprise, this is one of the advertisements I saw.

I don't believe that hair is, was or will be everything. I don't believe that any single part of your body can be a sole representative for who you are as a person. You may have features that accentuate beauty and grace your appearance, but that one feature or even ten of them doesn't make you whole. You are more than what you look. You are how you think, talk, love, laugh, and cry. Basically, you are a complex amalgamation of wonders called the human body, mind and energy. Cheers to this thought I say.

I know that appearances are important. First impressions can turn out to be last impressions. However, appearances cannot take such precedence that you start making them an undetachable part of your personality. Though it can be a part of your personality, it cannot be your complete personality. You are so much more than your hair, skin, eyes, and anything else that is visible to others. You are all that you are visible to *you*. How you see yourself is how others see you! Marisa Peer says, '*The most important words you say in your life are the words you say to yourself*'. If you say to yourself, you are not good-looking enough that is what you will believe. It's very unfortunate that we don't see our true selves. We want to be what others would like to see us as or even worse, we try to live up to what others think of us. The tendency to gratify others first and to seek validation from others is present in a lot of us. There were present in me for a large part of my twenty's. But there are more common in mothers! Yes, have you ever seen a mother tell her child to not disturb her while she is reading, watching her favorite show, or even eating her food? As a matter of fact, every time my friends who are mothers sit down to have their meal, their child needs to poop! About she goes and helps the child out, leaving her food to get cold. The glorified pretext that God couldn't be everywhere so he made mothers, has put mothers on some superhuman pedestal where even Wonder Woman, if she had babies, would fall short. Or wait, does she have babies that I don't know of? What one forgets is very important and the biggest truth about a mother - that she is human and that she has her needs.

As I was mentally mocking this advertisement, my phone started flashing Mira's name. Mira usually does not call early in the morning hours, because she is cooking, packing lunch boxes, making tea, talking to the maids, and cleaning up last night's mess that the children have made. I picked up the phone to hear high pitched screaming, the pressure cooker in the background, and the TV on which the IPL match was playing. I had to take away my ears from the phone or my first visit would be to an ear surgeon's clinic and not my own.

"Hi! I am sorry. A lot of things happening today!" Mira had gone to a bedroom to get away from the chaos. "What's up M?"

"*Arre yaar*, I need to see you today!" She said against the backdrop of her young one who had followed her screaming into the room.

"Yeah sure, come in today, I'll make time. By when…" and she hung up on me before I could fix a time. This Mother Hen was mothering not only her children but her entire household. She did come, after seven days. That's another fact about mothers, their urgent matters translate to the last thing-to-do on their list. Before that, it's everyone else's thing-to-do. Her 'today' came on the seventh day- a Sunday. I love my friends, I do, and don't get me wrong, but a Sunday is sacred to me. It's my book day, spa day, sleep-in day, and chocolate day! Sundays to me are all about me! I did not crib though, because I loved Mira more and decided that we meet for a fancy brunch at a beautiful restaurant in a cozy suburb of Mumbai. I got up, all excited, picked out a cute dress with my favorite bird pattern on it, wore light make-up, did my hair, wore the new heels I had gotten last week, and stepped out.

The weather was enthralling. The monsoons had begun, and the streets were reflecting mosaic patterns of water. The smell of wet earth reminded me of my grandmother's watered garden. Have you noticed that the birds chirp happier in monsoons? You must if you haven't. I promise, if you hear close enough, you might even hear a *Hum aapke hai kaun** tune at times or even a *Saat samundar paar** tune. By the time I had identified an ABBA and a Michael Jackson song in the chirps as well, I had reached the restaurant. I saw Mira's silhouette through the large glass window. I picked up my pace and entered the restaurant with a huge smile, to see a completely different Mira than what I had imagined. You remember the feeling when you get invited to a party and you are the only one overdressed? I felt like I had come to someone's funeral dressed like an Indianized version of Beyonce. I hugged her and sat down.

"You look great!" Mira said with a warm smile.

"Thanks, and you look tired." I had to be honest with her. Her dark circles had created dark halos around her eyes. The chubbiness of her cheeks was lost. Her skin looked dry, and she had started to develop age spots. Her cute curly hair wasn't curly anymore. It looked frizzy, dull and straw-like. And when I noticed closely, I could see some parts on her scalp where her hair had thinned out.

"Psst… Can you peak in here?" she whispered breaking my chain of thoughts.

"What is it?" I shifted a little so that I had a good view of what she was holding in her bag. "Take it out," I said not able to see what she was holding.

"No!" Her answer was so loud that someone would have thought I was carrying contraband in it. I had to get up and peer inside. It was a zipper bag full of hair. I was glad she hadn't held it out in the restaurant.

I get a lot of women, who get zipper bags, with their fallen hair. The zipper bags are of good quality, and the hair is bad. The sight of the entangled mesh of dead dry hair doesn't affect me anymore. This gesture is a symbol of how frustrated the patient has become, and I, therefore, keep my feelings aside and focus on the patient. "Is this the urgent

        famous Bollywood songs

matter?" Her thinned-out scalp, which I had noticed a while back, flashed in my mind.

"Yeah, I want you to see but not here. And I tried to come to the clinic, but I couldn't. I didn't have time because Zia came and demanded that I make her fruit salad with custard, and looking at that Abram started howling for biryani…"

"And you made all of that last minute?" I was astounded by the amount of energy this tiny woman could have in her. I know size doesn't matter when it comes to energy. Kids are the perfect example. But here was this woman in her mid-30's doing everything, for everyone, all the time, every day. She continued to talk. "Then Dad came and said he wanted to go to the bank. Took him there. Manish asked to look at a resume that he had written. And then…"

It had become so exhaustive for me to keep track of her responsibilities that I had zoned out. "That's why you look tired," I stated as a matter of fact. "Why don't we order something and talk it out in a while. I'll tell you how we can treat it. Sound good?"

"Three Bloody Mary's!" she yelled to the waiter with an emphasis on the word bloody. Her brains were probably more bloodier at this point.

"Gosh, I am so lost and stuck…" came her statement in the middle of a conversation we were having about Bryan Adams. I was trying to empathize. That was the only thing I could do. "I mean… I know I chose this life. I loved singing and then gave up on it because I wanted to start a family. Manish kept insisting that I didn't have to pause my career but no… I made a choice. I decided to pause. I hate this life!" A tear rolled down her left cheek. The clinking of the cutlery on plates, and the occasional loud laugh from another table were a stark contrast to what was going on in Mira's mind. She was in a dark place. "I am such a bad mother to say such things!" She covered her eyes to hide her embarrassment.

I looked at her with compassion, "No, you are a human

first. And you can allow yourself to say that." She had fallen for the same farce that so many women fall for: A mother is Wonder Woman.

We have grown up watching role models like our mothers, grandmothers, our friends' mothers, and Bollywood mothers like Reema Lagoo, who have been epitomes of sacrifice. Therefore, our subconscious minds cannot fathom any mother behaving otherwise. The template of The Ideal Mother is deeply ingrained in our brains. The influence of this template is so intense that, we too want people to see us as The Ideal Mother. As ideal as the world defines it and nothing less. We believe that it is the only right way to go ahead. But we forget to understand, rather we are not taught to realize, that these very role models before being mothers, were also people. Living breathing people with their thoughts, feelings, ideals, and ambitions. And, because of this ignorance, we fail to realize that motherhood is but only a role played by a woman. These role models, then become our way towards self-destruction, exhaustion, burn out – call it whatever you want. I moved up next to her and put my arm around her shoulder. Her tears continued to wet her shirt. I could feel a subtle shiver run down her body.

"How many times have you called your mother by her name?" I asked her.

She looked at me with confusion. "Never… Why would I call her by her name?"

"Answer the question. What's her name?"

"Leena, but Why are you asking about my mom?"

"How many times have you called your mom by her name Leena?"

Her irritation was starting to show. "That would be disrespectful." She answered.

"But she was Leena, way before you were born, before she got married, and had you. She was Leena, a person, a girl who grew into a woman, way before you even knew of her existence. She has had her ups and downs, she has had her laughs and heartaches, she has a favorite flavour of ice cream and Ranbir Kapoor is probably who she crushes on. Maybe, this person Leena loved to sing and dance, she loved how the rains made her heart sing and how she loved to smell the roses. The morning sun was her delight and the crisp winter mornings were her favorite time of the year. She is a person with the name Leena. And her identity got lost as yours did behind the role of a mother." Her sad eyes looked at me. But there was poetry visible in them. The sort of poetic sadness that reveals a glint of hope, a dawn of a new understanding. "Like she is a person called Leena, you are a person called Mira. The world may forget who you are. But you need to remind yourself of your needs that need fulfilling, because no one else will. And this doesn't make you selfish. It shows that you have your self-interest at heart. Selfish and self-interest are different. Selfishness can prove to hurt someone else. But self-interest is all about getting to do things that you'd like to do without hurting the interest of others. Ensuring self-interest makes you compassionate, because it teaches you how to love and accept yourself without any pre-approved notions. And one of the biggest truth there is, a universal truth, is Love. If you know how to love yourself, you will know how to love others. It is never the other way round. This world taught us love- but it forgot to tell us how to love. We learned to receive love from others. We learned how to give our love to others. But we never learned how to love ourselves. Do you know what loving yourself does? It leaves you fulfilled in a way no one else's love can make you feel. It *defines* the feeling of love for you. Then, your need to be loved by others stops being a need, because you have fulfilled this need yourself. And when you feel fulfilled, you are ready to give. Give because you now have so much to offer. You are the eternal pot of food that Draupadi received. Any guest that came to the Pandava's house would never return empty stomach. I like to think of this pot that generated love, not food as in the mythology. It was unending love that Draupadi offered.

When we fill ourselves with love, we can give love to others in a wholesome way. And isn't that what is being a 'good' mother?"

Mira's sniffles continued. Her red eyes continue to overflow with tears as I continued. "Self-interest doesn't mean manipulation. It doesn't mean putting your needs before someone else's need when they need it more than you did. It is a way of putting yourself before others when others' needs can wait. How one does it, is their choice."

That day Mira did a lot of thinking and talking. She reminisced her yesteryears. She dreamed for a wholesome future where everyone's self-interest would be considered.

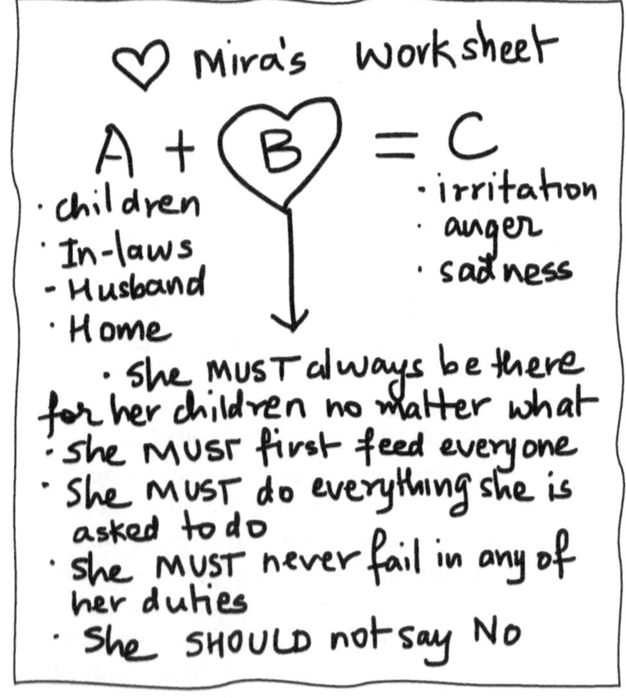

Fig. 8.1- Mira's worksheet

Mira was now going to take out an hour every day for herself, where she would be in her room with the door locked and sing. Only sing. No phones, no children, no cooks or maids, and no fathers or husbands would be there with her. Because, she wouldn't be a mother, a daughter in law or a wife in that room. She would keep aside The Ideal Mother template to adorn at a later time of the day. She would, in that one hour, be Mira. The person that she had forgotten she was. She would selflessly be only Mira. Now when did selflessness become selfishness?

J K Rowling was a mother too. A single parent at that, with a small girl to take care of and with no money. She still wrote her book Harry Potter- rather 7 books- that became best sellers grossing millions of dollars in revenue. Do you think she could write her book without having self-interest? And what did come out of that selfishness? A million-dollar idea, that sold millions of copies and made her and her daughter live happily ever after. Imagine if J K Rowling would have only run behind her daughter, fussing over her, keeping an eye on everything, and offering her services only as a mother? No one would benefit. Neither her daughter nor J K or the world! If self-interest meant doing things that benefited so many others, then I would also choose self-interest as well. I have chosen self-interest as I write this book for you. Michelle Obama has said, *"Being a mother has been a master class in letting go. Try as we might, there's only so much we can control. And, boy, have I tried — especially at first. As mothers, we just don't want anything or anyone to hurt our babies. But life has other plans. Bruised knees, bumpy roads, and broken hearts are part of the deal. What's both humbled and heartened me is seeing the resiliency of my daughters."* J K Rowling and Michelle Obama certainly did not follow a certain pre-made Ideal Mother Template as far as I see it. They made templates that suited them. Templates that allowed them to work efficiently. Efficiency allows one to enjoy the template irrespective of the outcome. An efficient person can seem to be a super-person, but inside the super-person's mind run emotions that are conducive to enjoying the process of performing the task, also called process enjoyment, rather than waiting to rejoice upon the success of the task, called task outcomes. Superhood leads to the rise of harmful emotions, that which border irritation, disappointment, anger, and sadness. Superhoods or supermoms expect fixed outcomes that suck the joy out of the process of being a mother. The obstinate demand of the child eating all the food served supersedes the actual joy of enjoying with your child over the table no matter how much it eats.

The afternoon sun shone through the window of the restaurant. It highlighted Mira's lovely curls and sparkled through her eyes creating a shimmer that I hadn't seen in a long time. "But how do I say No if the kids come and ask me for something. What if dad asks me something? I can't say No to him," she exclaimed.

No, is the shortest, smallest word that I know of. And yet it the hardest to utter. I see a lot of patients struggle to say it at the right time. To be honest, there is no right time to say No. There never was. There is not a 'NO pill' in the market that can give you the courage either. No matter your calculations, you cannot make it sound pretty or polite to people. What you can do is use polite words when framing your sentence. Rather that is all that you can do. By articulating your No in a manner that can help the person in front understand and ease out the blow. Because as much as you are not used to saying no, people around you aren't used to hearing a No from you. The funny part is, these same people who cannot hear a No from you, are likely to be experts in saying No to others. No, the word, doesn't mean *never ever*. It means 'No, to *that* person at that point in time'. Meaning, we take a No from our loved one personally, like an insult or a reprimand, when in fact it isn't. It is just a word that was used to communicate a mindset with no intention of offending. Mira had to unlearn her Yes and relearn her No.

No also means, that you are important for yourself at that point in time and others need to know it. And here comes the tricky part. If you were a Yes person like Mira and when you start saying no, no matter the language you were using, you would see people around you reacting like they are in the centre of the Katrina storm. At first, they may find it weird or even rude or outright insulting. They may think you have become arrogant and selfish. They may make you feel guilty by grabbing attention or by emotional blackmail. But the ones who matter, will stick around and see the butterfly come out of the cocoon. *They* will change their view of you because you changed your view of yourself. Because like you, they are people of habit too. They need time to adjust. They are people with their irrational belief systems as well. Some belief systems that you helped create in them with your yes habit. And as much as the road to change is full of dislike and discomfort, it's filled to the brim with happiness at the end. No? Yes? You will see!

"Can I get you some tea?" the waiter asked. "Thank you, but No." I said politely looking at the clock. My no didn't mean that I will never ever have tea did it?

"See it's easy to say NO... no?" Mira said with excitement.

"Hey, you didn't give me medicines?". She had long forgotten what she had come for. I had already slipped a prescription on the pen and paper that I carry around hoping that she had gotten more than what she had come for in the first place.

In his book, The Art & Science of Rational Eating, Dr Albert Ellis was very clear when he said, *'Life is indeed difficult, partly because of the real difficulties we must overcome to survive, and partly because of our own innate desire to always do better, to overcome new challenges, to self-actualize. Happiness is experienced largely in striving towards a goal, not in having attained things because our nature is always to want to go on to the next endeavor.'*

We are always in search of self-gratification and gratification from others. We strive to do better, be better and achieve more. And in this endeavor, we have stereotyped ourselves into different templates. The Ideal Mother template is the classic example but isn't the only one we know of. We have templates for everyone around us – Fathers, Brothers, In-laws, Family, Friends, Best Friends, Society, Neighbours, and even for a Dog. We don't like barking dogs, we like dogs who are needy and love us. Scooby doo is loveable for a reason you know! We put our near and dear ones in these templates and expect them to behave in a certain manner. We also put ourselves in these templates if we are playing a certain role in the society that we are a part of. I often do see myself as The Ideal Daughter and end up feeling guilty for not doing enough, more often than not. Varun had put himself in The Ideal Father template. Mira was The Ideal Mother, The Ideal Wife, and was also Ideal Daughter-in-law. Hard as it is to fulfil the expectations of others, the most difficult expectations to fulfil are those from the self. Like Varun and Mira, Nihar had put himself in The Ideal Son/ Activist/ Environmentalist/ Animal Lover template and whatnot. He had put himself on a pedestal so high, with so many expectations from the self, that in a way he had set himself up for failure rather than success. The process enjoyment was getting lost in this endeavour and the task outcome was taking precedence in life. And his facial pigmentation was speaking loud and clear of what this distress was doing to him…

9

Nihar's Facial Pigmentation Story
Be diplomatically responsible, and responsibly diplomatic

*The emotionally mature individual should completely accept the
fact that we live in a world of probability and chance, where there are
not, nor probably ever will be, any absolute certainties, and should
realize that it is not at all horrible, indeed—such a probabilistic,
uncertain world.*
~ Dr Albert Ellis

I sat stupefied. The red, blue, and white colors flashed on the screen. Like a moth to a flame, I was glued to the TV. My friend Nihar was on the screen speaking with passion about how he had worked with the farmers to fight the local panchayat and help them start their water supply- an irrigation plant. A farmer who would have access to water, as much as he wanted, throughout the year, was unheard of. He spoke with fervour about how his effort was only a drop in the ocean and how he would continue to make more irrigation plants. The happy farmers standing behind him all nodded their heads in unison. This was just the beginning and for the better.

I for one, have always been awed by people who follow their passion. And as much as I hate to admit it, with honesty I confide, that I still don't think I have found my true passion. Yes, I have been very diligent about my career. I run my clinic. I have my ups and downs when I meet patients. And on most days, I go home as a content doctor, who was able to help someone overcome their skin disease or insecurity about how they looked. But at times, I also go home defeated, when that one odd recalcitrant case shows up that isn't getting healed, or who refuses to admit that inner work is needed to help achieve remission or is unable to comprehend that doctors can only help and not 'fix' their bodies. Those are the times I am sapped due to the responsibility that I, as a doctor, take up on behalf of the patient. For those of you who haven't yet figured it out here is the truth: For every pill or injection the doctor has given you, she/he has taken on your responsibility if anything goes wrong. The good that happens to you, however, is the patient's doing. The patient is responsible for the healing that happens. Imagine the number of burden doctors as people go throughout the day seeing so many patients and yet greeting everyone with a smile and positivity. We have become so good at hiding our stress, that people have started to beat us up thinking we are 'irresponsible and careless'. I have felt exhausted taking up such responsibility at times. And here I was seeing Nihar, taking up huge responsibilities for others, almost as if he were the father to all those farmers and his actions would give them a better future, and still not tiring. He was working, inventing turbines, figuring out how to cajole the local authorities, and having excellent diplomatic relations with everyone around.

Now being diplomatic isn't as bad as you think. Truth be told, it isn't bad at all. Diplomacy is an art and I tell everyone around me to hone this art. Diplomacy doesn't mean you get your evil way. It means, with your skills of communication, you and the person in front, both get benefited by meeting in the middle. Diplomacy is often confused with the word exploitation or manipulation. Manipulation is all about getting only your way by causing harm (albeit not in the literal sense) to the person you are dealing with. I go a step ahead and say, that all relations are diplomatic. Psychologist Dr Paul Hauck has written a book with the title *'Marriage is a Loving Business'.* Even the relationship between a mother and a child is a loving yet a diplomatic business. And it must be that way because it works. Every time you put a rule in front of your child, no matter how beneficial it is for them, has your child accepted or resisted? Imagine using diplomacy. Both of you get your way. For e.g., how would you tell a five-year-old and a sixty-five-year-old that candy is bad? Would you use a different tone, use different words, and gestures? Yes, of course you would use different styles of communication, unless you were a robot. Diplomacy helps.

Nihar was always the diplomatic one among us, helping him garner so many friends in so many fields. And these friends were people who would go to lengths to help him out because their help was reciprocated by Nihar with the same zeal as theirs. In a way, such diplomacy, or as I like to call it- nobility, increases your sense of responsibility. Because when people do things for each other with a good heart, people start to matter. There develops a sense of responsibility towards each other. It's a loop- call it a vicious one or helpful one.

Nihar loved his friends. He had helped Varun and had helped me too. And I always wondered how he did it all. And as much as diplomacy mattered, it could take you only short distances and here is where his passion stood out. Nihar had found his burning desire and that is what kept him moving. However, contrary to his zest, his face had darkened around his temples and his cheeks. The dark circles around his eyes make him look tired and even angry at times. I could see furrows as deep as valley's on his forehead. And his hair reflected white light as he spoke to the reporter standing in the sun. Here was a man, following his passions, living his life, eating wholesome fresh foods, breathing the freshest air there was, and yet he had started to show signs of a pigmentation-like condition called Acanthosis.

Acanthosis is the thickening of the skin, not pigmentation as most assume. It occurs over the temples, cheeks, and even around the mouth especially in men. Women aren't exempt. The thickening of the skin can occur around the neck as well. The skin can become so thick, that one can see a dirty warty band of growth. Underarms and groins can also get affected. And this condition happens due to the increase in body fat, not sun exposure. The biggest myth there is about such pigmentation is that it is due to tanning. If I were to get a rupee every time a person called acanthosis a tan, I would be a Crorepati. When the body fat increases, the insulin in the body cannot function well. When the insulin cannot do what it is supposed to do- burn food- it starts acting elsewhere on the body. And insulin is a very hard-working hormone. It's like that dude in your office who once starts work, will leave only when he finishes his job. This insulin will find something to do once it leaves the pancreas and is out in the bloodstream. It won't while away time or go back home to the pancreas. And since it makes things, it starts making extra skin in the form of pigmentation and even small mole-like eruptions on the body called skin tag's or DPN's.

And it is very different from pigmentation or dark skin. If you ask me, I adore the skin color. Light or dark, no matter the shade, the color of the skin imparts an elegant character to your personality. Nyakim Gatwech, the woman with the darkest skin in the world, was once asked by a taxi driver to 'bleach her skin'. We Indians bleach even when we are not the darkest skin type in the world, all due to the fear of being labeled as *kali or kala**. The Indian society has overcome this prejudice to an extent, but we still have a long way to go till we start seeing more Nyakim's in our society.

I was seeing these changes of acanthosis in Nihar as he spoke. Ironically, *my* belief of how a wholesome life *must* lead to good health was getting challenged. As far as I remember, he didn't have a heart history or any diabetic history in the family. His family health was good. His genes weren't responsible, but epigenetics seemed to play a role. I couldn't guess how despite having a great country life, epigenetics would cause his condition. My dilemma continued throughout the day. But it didn't last long, because Nihar turned out to be a mind-reader and called me to invite me over to the farm. Thrilled with his invitation, I

                    dark-skinned

accepted it with joy.

The next day I was

on my jolly way. I reached his farm in the wee morning hours to be welcomed by a breath-taking view of the landscape. All of nature was welcoming the winters. The early morning dew on the grass reflected the tender sunrays like crystals. The cows mooed and the rooster frolicked, singing cock-a-doodle-doo till it reached ecstasy. The hens ran around with their chicks and the horse neighed as they played. I parked my car and went inside.

"Welcome Doctor *Sahiba**!" Nihar yelled and hugged me.

"I am jealous!" I slapped his shoulder. "Gosh, I hate you!" It was the most endearing thing I could say to him because I was feeling a pang of envy.

"I didn't expect you could kill me with such honesty," said Nihar, "and in that case, I hate you too!"

The tea was rich and creamy with fresh milk from the buffalo called Chameli from his stable. "Varun said I should name her Chameli- after you!" Nihar joked.

"Why?" I asked laughing out loud. The whole idea of a buffalo christened after me was comical. No one had or nothing had been named in my honor so far. Only my mother had called me names like *rani, beta, moorkh,* and sometimes even *gadhi* over the years. He got up with air of seriousness and stood next to me. He put his arms around my shoulders and said pointing out to the buffalo Chameli, "Can't you see the striking resemblance?

I pushed him away as he laughed. I loved animals. Any type, anywhere, and at any time. If you were to hand over an animal in my lap amid a storm, I could end up playing with it forgetting that I had to save my life! It makes me wonder, if I were better off as a veterinary doctor. Could that be my true passion I wondered every time single time I encountered an animal. Dogs and horses were my favorite kind. I pet the top of Chameli's head and we moved on to see Nihar's farm.

"Saheb! Saheb! Tya Sarpancha cha phone ala ahe…!" Came a farmer running towards him. *"Pumpatla pani band jhalay, shetala keed lagli ahe ani Saraswati la bara nahi ahe."* The head of committee had called complaining that the irrigation pump wasn't working, some of the crops were infested, and that Saraswati wasn't well'. I was stupefied by all these issues this man had come with. And they all seemed like priority-based issues to a layman like me.

"Who is Saraswati?" I asked.

"The Cow. She isn't well it seems," said Nihar with concern. "She hasn't been keeping well for some time." He gave multiple instructions to the man, all with patience. There was no whiff of frustration or irritation in his tone or demeanor. If I hadn't had learned psychology, even as a doctor I would have lauded his capacity to keep calm in such intense situations. The small adrenaline bursts that his body was undergoing as he spoke with such poise did not go unnoticed by me. Our mind is a miracle. Its job is to fish out threatening situations and avoid them in order to say safe. As Dr. Joe Dispenza, the author of the book called *Becoming Supernatural* says, in the earlier years, when we saw a tiger, our mind would instruct our body to secrete adrenaline- which is responsible for the fight-flight-freeze mechanism of the body. Once we ran away from the tiger and were sure that it wouldn't be anywhere near, we settled down and our adrenaline levels came back to normal. This Tiger is perceived as a biological threat to our existence by our mind and through appropriate changes in the body we *physically react* to this threat by away or hiding.

A reaction is a spur of the moment action, unthought of and unrehearsed, which is carried out when we perceive a biological threat to our lives. In the example of the Tiger, we saw it and ran. Imagine if we had taken time to contemplate and plan out our escape route, we would happily do so from inside the stomach of the Tiger. Now this planning is called as a *response* and applicable to psychosocial threats or mini-tigers as I like to call it. And we are facing these mini-tigers each day of each week of every month every year, year after year in the form of jobs, wars, neighbours, animals, humanity, and the list goes on. These mini-tigers have become a metaphor for psychosocial threats and we are still reacting to them and not responding to them as is expected of us if we are to live peacefully. And as we confuse biological threats with psychosocial threats, our mind perceives them as a threat to our existence leading to the secretion of adrenaline into our blood stream. Because we aren't developing appropriate responses to these psychosocial threats, we aren't letting our adrenaline levels settle down. And like the ever so sincere insulin hormone, adrenaline is also another warrior molecule. It will do what it's supposed to do and even more. If you remember the flow chart in *Fig. 6.2* - Adrenaline also caused the skin to thicken and increase pigmentation.

Nihar heard it all out. Living on the farm had added years of maturity. The unconditional acceptance of the fact that Nature has her ways and that She cannot be controlled had added furrows on his forehead that screamed worry. His laugh lines pointed to having relinquished his beloved ray bans. His hair was all faded and gray. The sunlight had carved its presence on his face but Nihar was proudly showing it off. His hard work etched for everyone to see. But though his mind felt satisfied, his body wasn't coping up.

The mind is a very sly thing. The *Veda's* say that you are not your body. Because if we were our body, then we would have been able to control our breathing! But we can't decide to stop breathing and live can we? There is a mechanism in place that is making the act of breathing passive. There is the passive action of the heart beating. There is the passive action of your hair growing, menstrual cycles or even feeling hungry. These mechanisms are proof that we are not in control of our bodies as we thought we were. There are certain circuits between the brain and organs like lungs, heart, stomach, uterus etc., that are working round the clock, unbeknownst to us. In the same manner, we are also not our mind. Because remember the Automated Negative Thoughts - ANTs? These ANTs are happening when we are unaware. We cannot control these harmful thoughts. We can divert ourselves from these thoughts by having an occasional ice cream, watching a favorite movie, or even going out to a party. But can we, with our mindfulness stop them completely? We have allowed our minds to make puppets out of us. We are running on auto-mode, letting many auto-thoughts affect us. Because that is what our mind has told us.

In Nihar's case, his mind was ruling him. There is a thin line between passion and obsession. Both are good and equally needed. However, your body doesn't understand your passions or obsessions because you are not your body and your body is not you. Your body needs rest as *it* demands. And hear ye! Your mind also needs to switch off. You are the driver, and your body is your car. You can't expect the car to keep moving for 24 hours, even if you wanted it to. We have to realize that our bodies are 'things'. Separate entities. Like we take care of our phones and laptops so diligently- we don't take care of ourselves as much as we should. Having one spa day or one vacation doesn't mean you are respecting your body and giving it rest. Your body and mind need rest every day.

This self-destructive behavior arises because we were not told how to treat ourselves with respect. We want people to acknowledge us, appreciate our efforts, validate us, even love us for all we do for them. But the problem is that until we know how to acknowledge, appreciate, validate, and love ourselves first, we cannot expect the same behavior from others. This is a hard concept to understand, especially because we live in the land of Rama, Mahabharata, Sati's, and Sita's, where a sacrifice was the ultimate goal, pleasing others was the only duty, and being righteous was the supreme mantra for achieving *moksha*. Of course, our views are changing. Methodical and metaphorical analysis of these magnificent texts by authors like Devdatta Pattanaik are helping us change our perspective towards the art of interpretation. But as a doctor, I believe the change is happening at a snail's pace. In our land of sacrifices, both men and women are expected to give up or change their dreams because of the responsibility they hold for others. And it is for this reason that they have forgotten to learn how to draw the line. I like to cite the example of the Laxman-Rekha here. The line that Laxman drew for Sita, was in fact, meant for Ravana as well. When Ravana, disguised as a poor saint, comes to ask Sita for alms, she gives it to him from behind the line that Laxman has drawn. But when Ravana demands that she cross the line and give her the alms, she is reluctant. She knows his expectation from her is not justified. But she crosses the line anyway because she doesn't want Ravana to curse her or her family. After all, she thinks that it is her *dharma*. I always wonder, when I hear this story, how did it matter from where Sita gives alms to Ravana. As long as she did her duty with respect by handing over alms to him, it was fine. Why was she expected to give alms to him as *he* demanded? As I see it, here is where Ravana crossed Sita's comfort line and blackmailed her instead. For me, it is not a symbol of female oppression or modern-day sexism. Not only was Sita expected to not cross this line, but even Ravana was not to cross it either. My interpretation of the Laxman Rekha stands thus: It marks as a sign of setting certain limits of expectations of others from you. This line has to be set by you and only you. In short, the moral of the story-- "Learn to draw lines between what you can do and what is expected of you!"

And who says responsibility is not good. If you are a father, yes you are responsible for your children or wife, or family. If you are a mother, you have your responsibilities and so on for all the roles you are playing. But have you ever wondered who is responsible for you? Isn't that a thought you should think at some point? It's a tough question, but does it not warrant an answer because you are also entitled to care, love, and respect from others. No matter the intensity of love you share with your closest people- how many times have you experienced someone standing up for you and saying something as simple as *'It's okay, I will take care of it?'* Is there a guarantee that this person who stood up for you the first time, will stand up for you all the time and every time? Like you are a human, so is your loved one who stood up for you. That loved one may be having a bad day when you want some support. The day you feel your spouse or your child should have behaved responsibly in a certain situation, that day could have been a bad day for your spouse at work and a bad day for your child at school. Only you are responsible for yourself. You need to show up for yourself, always, every time, no matter what. Nihar was showing up all right, for everyone else but himself. His cows, goats, plants, crops, farmers and their families and their cows and goats and tractors and the weather and the water…. The list was endless. He turned towards me after he passed on a few instructions to the farmer.

"How do you not get tired of taking so much responsibility?" I asked with awe.

"I do. But if I don't do it who else will?" Nihar asked looking at the farmer run along for his tasks.

"What happens if no one does it? Is it the end of all that you stand for?"

He laughed loudly shaking his head sideways, like parents do when you say something that sounds childish to them. "Let's go," he said.

"Where to?" I smiled not letting the topic slide.

"Anywhere you want to go… there is this beautiful hill…"

"Will you come?" I interrupted, not letting go of the discussion I had started.

"Oi Mad Girl, I am here with you aren't I?" He slapped me on the back.

"No, you aren't," I said peering into his eyes. His

furrowed brows were visible from a kilometer away. "You haven't been completely present here with me... Have you realized you haven't stopped working since I met you?"

He flung his arms in the air, "If a goat is sick, I have to look into it, I can't let it die." He interjected. "And there are things on the farm that I can't push off to the next day or lives suffer – in the literal sense. But you wouldn't understand." This defence wasn't unexpected. He was lonely. He felt as if he was doing too much and that I wasn't supporting him.

Defences are wonderful systems to hide feelings of fear or loneliness. In my experience, defensive people aren't only angry people, but they are people who have become experts at hiding their insecurities. They aren't being inconsiderate of you. They are being human and hiding behind their fears, worries, or even feelings of loneliness. It is easy to be defensive than to face your fears. The responsibility that has been taken up by them are important to them. Or so their mind says. The mind doesn't want to feel fear or sadness or loneliness. Because that is against the instinct of survival. The biggest fear is that if I let go and feel these emotions, I will not be able to gather myself.

Nihar's fear was evident. He cared for his family of farmers. If you are the head of your family or live in a joint family, you have may related to this situation. But, you also need to take care of yourself- because in this case, in Nihar's case that is, he wasn't. And he wasn't allowing his family to take care of him. He wasn't delegating tasks to them. His reluctance to lose control over an engine that ran steadily otherwise, was causing him to take up work more than his mind and body could endure.

I looked at him and hugged him. I could feel his arms tighten around me in between his sobs. All the responsibilities he had endured for his family ran down his cheeks in tears. His sacrifices weren't sacrifices to him but they were more of a duty. A reason for his existence. A reason to have walked this earth.

"I am tired," he pulled away and said. "And I am getting sick. Look at me. My cholesterol is off the chart. I look like someone painted charcoal on me. Gosh, I look like I am 60 already!"

"We can fix that you know now?" I teased.

"How?"

"By fixing you!" I yelled.

"Man Chameli, *tu toh pagal ho gayi hai yaar**!" he chuckled.

I took my pen and paper and explained to him the A+B=C formula. On that hill, amongst the trees and in the

clouds, as it started to drizzle, Nihar worked in harmony with it all. The A's seemed to flow unhindered. His B's were being jotted down. His *must's* and s*hould's* had started to take shape on paper reminding him of things he needed to change. The freshness of the grass lifted his spirits. He, on occasion, put down his pen to smell the wet earth and to look over the valley. The occasional stray goat grazed the fresh grass almost eating the paper he was writing on. He looked at the goat with love and I looked at his face. The lines seemed to have eased out, like magic. As a dermatologist who also does toxins and fillers, when I see the marvel of self-realization take over a person's face, I am forced to think if we need these cosmetic procedures at all. The eternal fountain of youth that continues to exist in us can start creating magic by itself. When I hear stories of women at 70 who look like 50, I keep aside my analytical and skeptical mind and tell myself, maybe this lady found her fountain of youth by changing her B's and got to be evergreen and eternal again. Nihar was transforming. The feeling was palpable. I knew he had already started healing.

 **You have gone mad*

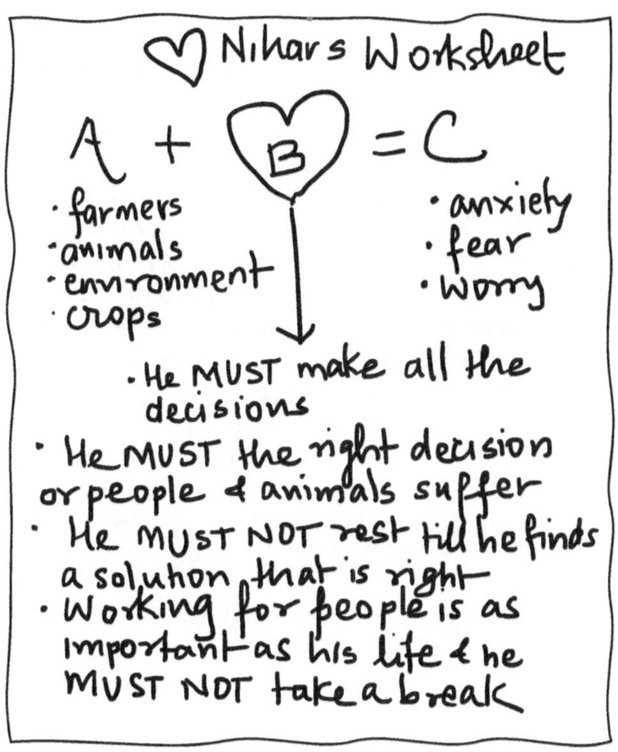

Fig. 9.1 Nihar's Worksheet

We got up and started walking downhill. Words seemed meaningless at the point. I walked aside him in silence, seeing him busy, reminiscing in his thoughts. As we reached the bottom, he picked up a stone that lay and turned towards me. "I was being too hard on myself. As much as I love this life and this life loves me, I need to take it easy. I had forgotten how to celebrate." He said with tear-filled eyes.

At that point, I knew that all the Chameli's and Saraswati's would start loving him even more. Because he had started to love himself.

Hasan Minhaj, in the last episode of The Patriot Act,

said, "*We as people are so affected by everything wrong that is happening around us. Animals are getting extinct, corporates are getting ruthless, the environment is in shambles, racism hasn't died, humanity is up for sale… there are all these tabs which are open in our mind's browsers. We need to shut some of them down, for our own sake.*" Let go. As much you care for the animals, the trees, the people, the society, democracy, education, poverty, climate change, you still need to choose which one it is that you would like to see changed, at least in this lifetime. For the other problems, let someone else take up the job for a change! Be a crusader, but it wouldn't harm you if you were a crusader who chose wisely your crusades.

As for me, my crusade has been helping people with their A's, B's, and C's. And my challenger Mr S who was the catalyst for my crusade to write this book was coming for his follow-up the next day...

10

Mr S's Psoriasis Story

The day I redeemed myself as a dermatologist

The words '*You cannot help me*' echoed in my mind. The consulting room seemed to provide comfort with its warmth and coziness. The gentle movement of the fan my consulting room, rustled the leaves of the money plant that had grown, as I had, over the years of my practice. But I wasn't at peace. Mr S was due for his follow-up today. I picked up a book by Dr Albert Ellis and started to read.

"You and many outstanding inventors and writers have striven for the ideal and have thereby helped yourself do remarkably well. REBT, therefore, does not oppose competition or striving for outstanding achievement. It advocates task-perfection, not self-perfection." "What does that mean?" "It means that you can try to be as good, or even as perfect, as you can—at any project or task...........

I looked up from the book with a knock on the door. Mr. S had finally come for the follow-up. I inserted a bookmark, a peacock green one which Raghav had gifted me and kept the book aside to read later. As Mr S entered my consulting room, he still seemed like a man who could use chilled ice cream to cheer him up. But he seemed a tad more uplifted than he was the last time he came.

"Your creams seemed to have helped," he said with a faint smile. "But the psoriasis hasn't completely gone!"

A lot of patients end up at the dermatologist with chronic diseases they have been carrying around for years and expect a complete clearance in fifteen days.

"I am sure the remaining will also fade as we go ahead with the treatment," I said.

He got up and proceeded to the examination table. His

lesions had started to subside. Some were almost gone. His ruddy face had turned into a healthier pink. The scales around his forehead had reduced showing signs of healthy skin. Years of psoriasis had taken a toll on his nails, but they seemed to be growing out healthy.

Mr S was a contractor. Taking orders from clients and working with carpenters, plumbers, electricians, etc,. A middleman that tries to please everyone so that people can live in their homes safely and happily. As much as he spread happiness through homes, he seemed very sad. His eye bags, stood out like cloves of garlic, adding another ten years to his age. The shine of his eyes that was missing the first time he came had returned, but not enough to ignite his happiness. He looked at my face without expressions as I examined him.

"There is improvement... *Accha hai.*" The lesions seemed to be healing.

"I know it is better doctor. It always gets better. But it always comes back too. My uncle's friend's wife's mother suffered from stage IV cancer and even she got better! I don't!" he retorted.

Here is the truth about diseases. Any disease. It manifests because of the choices you make and it heals because of the choices you make. You may not have a choice in what disease affects you, but you always have a choice in how to treat it. *Always.* This person with cancer had exceptional doctors and medicines but so do many other patients. She was given the same medicines there are to treat cancer like those many other patients did. Then how did she manage such a feat? Call it luck, but I like to replace the word luck by choice. I always tell my patients who suffer from skin diseases that they are luckier than most. Because at least they can see what their choices are doing to their body. For many, unless they have a heart attack or stroke or get fat or thin or faint, they don't know that they have a disease: Because they choose the wrong foods, jobs, or lives. Consider skin diseases like a big gateway to health, a first step towards other diseases, or like an alarm signal. For example, adult acne is the first step towards metabolic syndrome. A syndrome that consists of diabetes, blood pressure, and raised cholesterol. So, if you knew that you had adult acne, you now knew that it is a health issue and not only a cosmetic issue.

"How many years have you had psoriasis?" I asked.

"Twenty almost."

"Then let us give the medicines two months at least to act?" I joked and he wasn't amused.

"Have you worked on the homework I gave you?" I asked taking out my pen and paper.

He stared at the table shuffling on his seat. "Why haven't you done it?" I asked with earnestness.

"I don't think it will work," he said rudely, waving his hands in the air.

I had strengthened my defenses this time. "Looks like you don't want to heal?"

"I do! That is why I am here, aren't I?" His impatience was climbing.

"It seems like you still aren't here by choice and your friend has forced this on you, yet again." I stated. He stayed quiet. "In that case, you were right when you made a statement when we first met," I had put my pen down and stopped writing his prescription. A doctor too has limits to being word bullied. He was now crossing my *Laxman Rekha*.

"What statement did I make?" He asked with rising curiosity.

"That I cannot help you. I recommend-- you go to another dermatologist of your choice." The warm cozy consulting room turned into a silent cold confinement room. My breathing was audible. Here I was trying to help this gentleman, and there he was not acknowledging my efforts. The ticking of the clock wrecked my nerves further. "If you don't want to help yourself, I can't help you. Even if I give you the best and most expensive medicines to treat your psoriasis." I said this point-blank.

"Fine…" he muttered. The clock continued to tick. "What do you want to know?" he asked with an empty stare.

I picked my pen and paper and wrote down my favorite formula. His smug face remained as is.

"What are you feeling as we speak?" I asked him. His attention was on the formula that I had written. And the analytical mind that he was, the formula had made him curious. "We will get there," I said distracting him from the formula, "but I need you to answer the question. What are you feeling as we speak?"

"I am frustrated doctor," He couldn't think of anything else to say.

"Let me ask you another question- how many emotions can you name?"

He only stared at me with confusion, as if I had asked him a ridiculous question. I prodded him to answer. "What happens to you when you see something or hear something you don't like?"

"I hate it" he said.

"There you go! Hate is a type of emotion. Can you name a few more?"

His eyes had brightened. "Sadness, anxiety, fear, worry, irritation, greed, jealousy, envy, dislike, depression." He said staring out the window.

"Can you think of anymore?"

He bobbed his head sideways.

"You named seven emotions. There are 1700!" I stated.

The change of expressions on the faces of people when they find out that there are 1700 emotions, is like a beautifully choreographed dance of the facial muscles. It's like magic. Taking off years of wrinkles. It is like verbal botulinum I must say.

"Do you know what an ANT is?"

He laughed for the first time at the question I was posing. "*Chitti**!" he said, what we call an ant in Hindi.

"*Mungi* in Marathi!" I added another colloquial name for the ant.

ANT's are automatic negative thoughts that constantly arise in everyone's minds. These are like Activating factors - the A's- but created by your mind. As the word suggests, they are automatic. Remember when I mentioned earlier in Nihar's story that you are not your mind as per the *Veda's*? These ANT's generate in your mind without you even knowing it. And you are not your mind, because if you were your mind then you would be able to identify these ANT's and also stop them. How many of us can stop these ANT's?

I continued, "have you experienced a time when you were in a good mood and the next moment you had started feeling your heartbeats go up and your breathing become shallow? That is the precise moment that you were most likely experiencing the ANT- negative thought. This ANT was your A which was causing the C (Fig 5.1). You need to change your thought that you were thinking at that precise moment."

He was looking at me with a piercing gaze.

"Tell me, what emotion describes you best...? Under a difficult situation, which emotion arises in you?" I asked.

"Anger," he said without pause.

We were making progress. "Now listen to me carefully, would you like to change this emotion and get free from it?"

His *yes* was as if a big burden had lifted off his huge square shoulders that had slumped with years of responsibility. He was ready to let go of his anger. Letting go is a sign that you are ready to heal. I have seen this happen in far too many patients. Holding on to notions, the past, and things like 'what he said/ what she said', makes us lead crippled lives. Letting go of these thoughts suggests that you now have the power to move on and take the first step towards healing.

I finally explained to him the formula and asked him, "Now tell me Mr S, what is the most important activating factor (A) that makes you angry." To change his anger, we knew that we had to identify his thought or the circumstance or the incidence that triggered his anger. He looked mellow. "Is it a person or a thing or an event that still causes you suffering?" I probed.

"Yes… It was an accident," he said with disgust.

I have seen people carry years of regret and remorse and anger of ghosts of the past. Be it a statement a mother-in-law made to her daughter-in-law on the day of the wedding, or a loved one cracking a joke at your expense in public, or your father being hard on you when you scored less in exams. Accidents and physical trauma carry worse repercussions. There is always a sense of being the victim for 'no reason'. The Why Me syndrome can run high and for a long time. Years of self -victimization leads to further reinforcement of the belief that something that should have never happened to you, happened. Especially when you are at the receiving end. Your thoughts keep ruminating in your mind, because your brain has developed new neural circuits for this habit. Yes, self-victimization is a habit. And as I mentioned earlier, the brain and its circuitry work on a concept called neuroplasticity. If you have a habit of procrastination, you will strengthen the circuit that 'allows' procrastination and further procrastination will reinforce this circuit. It is a vicious loop and the 21-day habit-breaking method works. It takes 3 to 4 weeks to break old habits and reinforce new ones. Victims are highly addicted to such thoughts. Because their brains get the much-needed juice to run from the various chemicals that get secreted every time this circuit gets activated. Again, you are not your mind. Meaning your mind is lazy. Your brain is lazier. It is never going to wake up one fine day and say- 'Oh hey I am bored of thinking like a victim, let me think like a hero or a survivor!' Uh-huh, that ain't happening- unless you train your brain. That is why a 21-day habit-breaking training is needed, to develop survivor circuits or hero circuits or better yet, to develop circuits of forgiveness.

"When did it happen?" I asked.

"Twenty years ago." His breathing had shallowed. His

shoulders tightened and his palm had turned into a fist. The victim had finally started to talk.

"What is it that bothers you?"

"That woman, she came out of nowhere, hit my car on purpose. I was driving on the road and she just…"

"Go on…"

"She tried to make a scene as if I had run her over. She tried to extort money… There was a big police case and I was making the rounds of the police station up until the last two years! My life was never the same."

"Where is she now?"

"How would I know?" his anger seemed to be rising.

"What's her name?"

"Are you seriously asking me these absurd questions? I don't care what her name is and I don't remember."

"Who won the case?"

"I did…Eventually… It took twenty years, but I finally got it overruled." He had tears in his eyes. It was difficult for a tough man like him to show such vulnerability to me, whom he had accused of not being capable of helping.

"That was a wrong verdict," I said shrugging my shoulders.

He wiped his tears and was now looking straight at me. "I won Doctor! Finally!"

"For a case you have won, you don't seem in a joyous mood. You seem like you could go wild with rage if she stood in front of you as we speak. Where is the victorious feeling? I used to think victory is all about celebration and happiness."

He stopped in mid- animation as if struck by lightning.

"She won. You lost. She is sitting somewhere with not a care in the world about what happened. Assuming she was a thief or con artist, she did her 'job' for the day, failed, and went off looking for someone else. Assuming she was genuine, she got hurt, went off, and started living her life. She most likely doesn't even remember you and here we are sitting and spending precious moments of your life talking about a woman whose name you don't even remember and wouldn't even recognize if she stood in front of you."

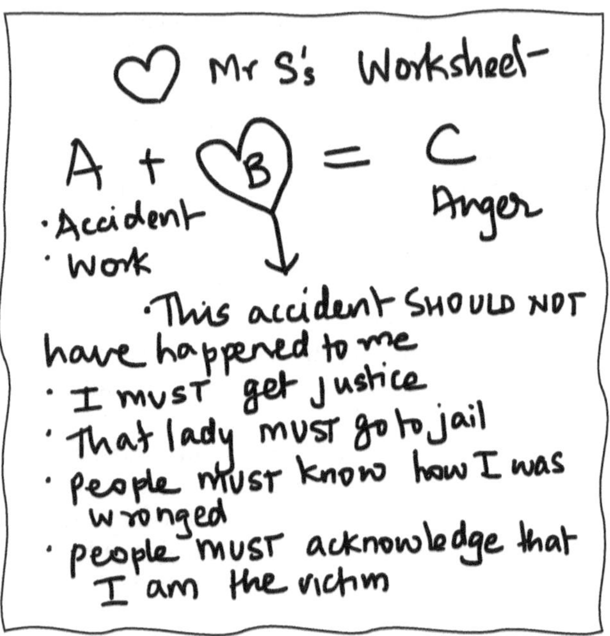

Fig. 10.1 Mr S's worksheet

Like I keep mentioning, there is a magical thing about realization. It is a moment of truth for most and for some it is a recognition of the lie that they were living. Mr. S had slowly started to understand how he had given his power over to a person he neither knew nor would ever know. They had crossed paths, and that was that. True, the path was rough. But it was in the past. How many times has anyone gone into their past and changed it? None. How many times did you wish that you could change your past? All the time.

For those with ruminating thoughts, also called *sticky* thoughts or *chewing gum* thoughts, you are letting your past affect your present moment. It is ruining your happiness in the present. And let's make a wild guess, what is going to happen to your future when you ruin your present? I won't answer this for you, because you know already. What matters is the present. Because I haven't learned the formula to turn back time. Neither had Einstein. And if I did figure it out – I would let you all in on the secret! Till then we are stuck with the Now. So, let's try to make the most of it.

"Do you know what is the most powerful tool to help your skin heal? Remember I had told you I would tell you the secret to heal your skin by yourself?" I asked.

"What?"

"Forgiveness." I smiled and left him alone with his thoughts.

For all those who know what forgiveness is, you know how relieving it is to let go. It seems easy for someone to advise forgiveness, but to the victim, it is the toughest thing to do. Believe me. I know. The biggest irony in life is this- the more you hold on to hatred or anger, the more the power belongs to the person who wronged you. And no, forgiveness is not reserved for the saints. They weren't born with different brains and with different neurochemical transmitters. They were born with the same serotonin, oxytocin, and dopamine that you, me, and everyone around us have. They reached sainthood because they knew how to secrete these neurotransmitters by regulating their thoughts. By reducing their ANT's. By training their brain to develop 'happy and forgiving' circuits, so much that they had mastered the brain circuitry for happiness, love, and forgiveness. And every time they did forgive, a surge of dopamine was let out into their blood stream which caused them to forgive even more. The surge of these feel-good chemicals surpasses all the weed, alcohol, and sex there is. It is addictive. And instead of being an addict to the hate chemical, they sought addiction to the forgiveness chemical.

"My wife tells me this all the time," he said smiling.

"Your wife is a saint," I said, and we ended the session

laughing.

Such moments give me a sense of subtle joy. Mr. S's journey had only begun. We both had a long way to go. But as Neil Armstrong, the first man to walk on the moon said, a small step turns out to be a giant leap, doesn't it?

I picked up the book by Dr Albert Ellis that I was reading and opened the page where I had stopped reading with a wide smile on my face...

"You and many outstanding inventors and writers have striven for the ideal and have thereby helped yourself do remarkably well. REBT, therefore, does not oppose competition or striving for outstanding achievement. It advocates task-perfection, not self-perfection." "What does that mean?" "It means that you can try to be as good, or even as perfect, as you can—at any project or task. You can try to make it ideal. But you are not a good person if it is perfect. You are still a person who completed a perfect project, but never a good person for doing so." "How, then, do I become an incompetent or bad person?" "You don't! When you do incompetent or evil acts, you become a person who acted badly—never a bad person."
~ Dr Albert Ellis

The bookmark that Raghav had given fell on the floor- I picked it up and placed it back in the book as it was. It was a reminder that I was going to meet him for dinner the next day.

11

Raghav's Atopic Dermatitis Story
How I stopped being an Enabler

Accept that acceptance is largely compassion — for you and yourself, for others and their self, and for the troubled world and itself.
~Dr Albert Ellis

Dr Albert Ellis says, *'Anger is the only emotion that people all over the world want to keep'.*

It is one of the best defence mechanisms known to man. It easy, simple, and effective. An angry person is feared by people around them. And that helps the angry young man to behave in the same angry manner over and over again. Much like the angry young man called Vijay Dinanath Chauhan, a character in a movie played by Amitabh Bacchan. Vijay's angry image proved to empower Amitabh Bacchan's image in real life, such is the power of anger. An angry man gets his job done. The people around him, who help him get the job done when he is angry, are Enablers.

Enablers are everywhere. Even I am an enabler when it comes to some people. The tantrum-throwing child who you want to whack on the bum is being enabled by his parents. As much as the parents want to avert the tantrum, they will try to mitigate the 'current' episode by giving in to the tantrum. But that is not solving the issue in the long run is it? It might stop the child from making a scene for the time being. But that child has learned the art of temper tantrums and will use this art it at a time when his parents are most vulnerable and have to give in to its demands.

Enablers are a common breed. Wives enable husbands. Husbands enable wives. Friends enable friends. People enable politicians.

Enabling can also be positive, in which case it is called reinforcement of a beneficial behaviour. When a child comes home with a trophy in drawing and the parents give him a pat on the back and say 'good job' - that is positive enabling. The child now knows that 'winning' is a behavior that can be inculcated. When husbands compliment their wives for the food cooked, and when the wives thank husbands for the money earned- that too is positive enabling. It helps develop relationships. It helps strengthen bonds.

Enabling doesn't mean letting people get their way under the guise that they mean a lot to you or because they are family. Such negative enabling can break or hurt relationships.

Remember Raghav? Yes, the rising-to-stardom cardiac surgeon from the Crazy Five. That's a lethal combination to deal with! And that's exactly why I twinged when I saw him calling. He was my friend, but we didn't see eye to eye on a lot of issues. We talked on rare occasions but that would be about a patient or two. His busy schedule as an upcoming bright cardiac surgeon didn't allow any room for 'frivolities' as he called it. Plus, as doctors, we were polls apart. He being the surgeon: No-nonsense, more action, less talk, and I being the physician: Common sense, necessary action, and lots of talk. It was like keeping a sheep and tiger in the same room and asking them to be friends. You know who the sheep is here.

I was meeting him over drinks. It seemed that he wanted to talk to me about his flared up eczema. I obliged and that's where the drama started. The setting was a beautiful rooftop garden restaurant that looked across the Powai lake. The rain had stopped for the day with the cool breeze blowing. The skyline of Mumbai was visible, a reminder of how She had grown vast, yet untiring in creating opportunities for all those who dared to dream. She was indeed the City of Dreams come true. A Wonderland. And I was Alice, never knowing what wish may come true and how.

"Hey," he said as he approached the table I was daydreaming at.

"How are you?" I smiled back.

"Perfect," came back his favorite reply. A word he never got tired of using, rightly so, considering the perfectionist he was. He signaled the waiter to come over.

"What is your poison? Or do you not drink in fear of getting a wrinkle?" He asked in a peevish manner. To think that he was in good mood, and I would enjoy the evening that was up, went down the drain. It was going to be one of the many irksome encounters that we had before.

"Why so glum chum?" He asked me after he had ordered for the both of us. My sullen face looked at his smug face which was beaming with a sadistic joy of having riled me up yet again.

"You tell me, you are the one who has the problem," I said taking a deep breath. He looked at me with an unflinching gaze and I stared back with equal intensity. We were a perfect example of how easy it is to communicate your precise feelings with silent stares. Our stare-feud got interrupted by the Whiskey Sour and Mimosa that the waiter placed on the table. I took the Mimosa and started sipping on it, trying to avoid further dialogue. My Circuit of Logic was on the verge of getting shorted. He sipped on his and smacked his lips.

"This…" He said pointing out to his rash on the hands and neck. He was suffering from atopic dermatitis for many years but had never felt the need to get treated by a dermatologist. His hands showed thick patchy skin at places. Dryness made the skin look flaky and red. His eyes seemed hollow due to the dark circles, and he seemed to sniff more often than not, because of the exacerbation of his allergies. "Moisturisers are my dermatologist," he mocked. By now, I was a pro at ignoring his sly comments.

My belief about people who make such comments is simple - they are insecure. They will have their own reasons for their insecurity. And the not-so-funny part is that they don't realize this one bit. He complained that the flares were now unremitting and worsening. His allergic asthma had flared up. The OT scrubs didn't help much either. And because he had to wash his hands often, they were turning dry. Applying even a bucket of moisturizer seemed less.

"You need to call 'steroid creams' your dermatologist," I said and folded my arms, "plus, I am sure you have stuffed yourself with oral steroids as well?"

He threw a fake grin at me. His signature grin that showed how he wasn't happy with the sarcasm. His hair created a pattern of waves on his temples, covering the slight gray that was now starting to appear. The dark circles that had started to show up were creating a tired look. His crisp white shirt looked crumpled from the day's work. His veiny hands rested on his folded knees, almost as if shutting himself from the rest of the world. 'This man's head must be like the Pandora's Box,' I thought to myself. As a surgeon, he was usually tired, and if not physically, mentally. After all, it is someone's heart he was dealing with all the time, and he couldn't afford to break it, pun intended. And being the angry young man he was, I was sure he didn't emote to anyone around him. He had never been vocal about his problems with me and any one of the Crazy bunch.

"No!" he said with irritation. I want to throw a disclaimer- doctors are generally pill-popping maniacs- because we can't afford to stay sick. We throw out the window all the routine meditation, the spiritual healing, and the long retreats to Bora Bora, and prefer the pill. It came quite as a surprise that he hadn't started himself on oral medicines. Although convincing him about oral steroids wouldn't be an issue, I feared that his issues were going to be deeper than it looked.

I looked at him and thew him a fake grin. "Remember

when you told me – it's not worth trying to change people - because unless they want to change they don't?" I asked. The confidence that a single Mimosa can bring is an absolute delight.

"Yes, and I stand by it," he answered with utmost animated conviction- very unlike the stone face he usually has. His Whiskey Sour was talking to my Mimosa now.

"What are your thoughts on changing yourself?" I dared to ask.

His whisky filled smile made his eyes shine bright, "That's possible! But difficult! Don't you think?"

"I didn't say it was easy." Pat came my reply! Hail the Mimosa! As much as it is hard to believe, but for a person who can rant on any topic in the world, I was usually tongue-tied in front of this man. Call it my defense or my tendency towards non-confrontation. Better yet, call me his Enabler. By enabling him, by being silent that is, and not contradicting him or challenging him, I avoided unpleasant situations around him. However today, the booze in me wasn't letting me enable him at all. The enabler was getting fuzzy and here was an opportunity at its ripe best to be plucked! "Gosh, you are so insecure!" I said with all my might the statement that I wanted to throw at him for ages.

He looked at me with shock. "Come on Manwatkar, control yourself!" he laughed hard.

I took a deep breath and smiled. "And the best part is that you don't even know it. I feel sad for you sometimes." I had overstepped my boundary, but it felt justified. Pitying a man such as Raghav is a dangerous task. Rather it is a foolish thing to do. It's like going and teasing a Tiger, 'Hey bro! You can't catch me and eat me!"

"Don't patronize me Pradnya," he said sternly.

"It is high time someone did," I said with a tone of authority putting a full stop to the enabler within me.

Imagine the tantrum-throwing child from the analogy I gave you at the beginning. What would happen to the child if its parents stopped giving in to its temper tantrums. It would cry, stomp, attack, scream, roll on the floor, and then what? This drama would go on for one min or five minutes or even one hour. But it would have to stop at some point, out of sheer physical exhaustion. And then how would the child behave? Quiet, tired, sullen, and very importantly- it would be in serious thought, in reflection, asking itself, 'What the hell happened?', 'Why did my plan not work (yes, kids can scheme!)?' It would get drenched in sweat and with shallow breaths would only be thinking of what went wrong. Raghav had gone through all these stages, albeit minus the childlike screaming and rolling on the floor. In his mind though, he was yelling, fuming, and screaming. And after he was mentally exhausted, he went quiet. He gulped down his drink and stared at me. I at him. To the novice we seemed like a couple very much in love, but lo behold, to the mindful eye- we were cutting each other's throats in our minds.

Here is what was happening in his blood stream: Every time he burst out into anger, his cortisol levels rose leading to changes in his immune system. There are various ways the immunity can get affected. Either it goes up or it goes down. The Immunoglobulin E/ IgE (a type of defense cell) levels can go up leading to all the symptoms of atopic dermatitis-like eczema, red eyes, asthma, and constant cough and cold. There is hyperactivity of the immune system that leads to an increase in the histamine levels and basophil overactivity thereby leading to the horrible itch *(Fig. 6.2)*.

We all like to say how things can cause allergies. How almonds gives hives or wine causes an itch or flowers are responsible for the sneeze. But where did this hypersensitivity come about in the first place? Now the question that plays is — do only angry people get atopic dermatitis? If you remember *Fig. 6.2*, any negative emotion can make your cortisol and adrenaline levels fluctuate. And I have consistently maintained that you cannot choose your disease, but you can choose your emotions, and you can further choose pleasurable emotions whilst discarding the harmful ones.

It took a while for him to calm down. He is a gentleman after all. I must admit that he was never the sort to abuse or walk out no matter how angry he got.

"Can I now talk and tell you exactly what needs to change in the least? Whether you want to change that part or not is up to you. I will not try to influence that." I finally spoke. He squirmed in his seat but agreed. I explained all that I had to tell him. The A's, the B's, and the C's to which he listened as the cool breeze ran through his hair and the setting sun highlighted the brown in his eyes.

His A's were his insecurities regarding his personal life and career, which were so deep rooted in him since childhood, that he hadn't realized them. Because he couldn't identify them, he couldn't change them. This led him to put up a facade of anger and sarcasm. People around him, because of his sharp tongue, never crossed him and that enabled him even more. His belief (B) - that 'he *must not* show his insecurities to others because they will see him as weak' had become his mantra. His belief that 'He *must not* trust people because they will only betray him' was only causing him harm. He hardly had friends and the people he surrounded himself with, he did not trust. It was a lonely life. A life where he had told himself he'd rather be a loner than let someone hurt him or his beliefs.

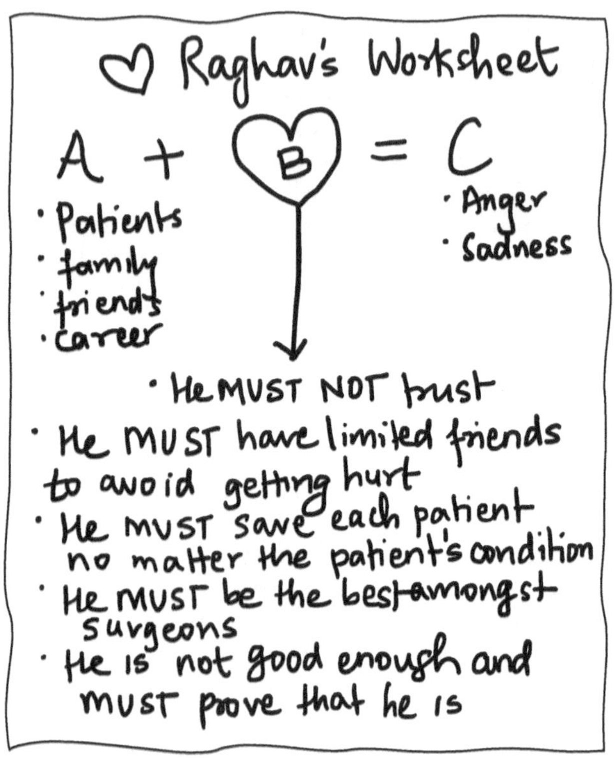

Fig. 11.1 Raghav's worksheet

Loneliness can be hard to deal with. One common misconception is that: Like a happy-go-lucky person cannot be lonely, an angry person likes his solitude. But nothing can be further from this misconception. Since it is hard to talk to the Raghavs of the world, people seem to avoid them. Why take the risk of being around the Angry Man whose Circuit of Logic shorts in the blink of an eye? No one likes to be at the receiving end of such a man. Talking to him is like trying to walk on eggshells. And thus, he is left alone, if not enabled. I have met such people and have also been at the receiving end of their wrath. But, owing to my commitment towards my relationships, I stay glued to their hair like chewing gum and have realized that these people are kind and big-hearted at the same time. If only they could identify their B's and change them, they could fill their lives with such unconditional joy that the happiest people would seem unhappy. On the rooftop restaurant against the backdrop of the City of Dreams, an angry man sat in front of me ready to open his heart to the kindness in him. A kindness that he owed to himself. The same kindness he showed his patients while he operated, would now be accessible to people around him too. Finally, in that beautiful twilight moment, I saw a kind man, the man that he truly was, shining with the grace of a healer that he already was.

Dr Albert Ellis said, *'As a result of my philosophy I wasn't even upset about Hitler. I was willing to go to war to knock him off, but I didn't hate him. I hate what he was doing."*

People aren't bad. But there can be people who do bad things. There aren't 'good people', but people who are capable of goodness. There isn't an angry person, only person who gets angry. A sad person is a person who is feeling sadness in *that* moment. Similarly, when it comes to abilities, there isn't a good painter, only a person good at painting. A child isn't a good kid because he scores good grades, only a kid who gets good scores. See the difference? We label everyone and everything, as in the case of Raghav. Bad guy, good guy, sad guy, ugly guy, good painter, bad kid…etc. It narrows down our capacity to see the vast many potentials that a person has and can explore. If I told a child that she was a good girl every time she scored well in mathematics, she would believe that the goodness of her being was linked to her scoring well in mathematicse. What if I told a child she was a girl who was good in mathematic? Wouldn't this open her realm and help her understand her potential in other areas like arts or science? If she is a girl good in maths, could she also explore her potential in the field of arts, science, sports, etc? It is easy for us to label people as good or bad or ugly or beautiful or stupid or intelligent. It is way more difficult to look beyond what we see and make an attempt to know a person based on the potentials in them. Maybe next time when you label someone as angry or bad, could you think to look at this anger or badness as only a trait that can be changed? A trait that isn't permanent? Because the only permanent thing is change.

Raghav's crumpled shirt reflected his crumpled spirit but the radiance of a healer that emanated seem to iron it out. He looked at years of B's that were showing through the manifestation of his atopic dermatitis. He smiled seeing the twilight and gazed towards the lake. The serenity of the lake reflected on his face. For the first time, he wasn't the man I knew him to be, different both outside and inside. He looked unified, in body, mind, and soul. Although his journey towards healing had only begun, he looked as if he was already healed. The Alice in me saw another dream being fulfilled in this Wonderland of relationships.

12

A+B =C- Change your skin story

The one formula for your skin to heal itself

What disturbs men's minds is not events but their judgments on
events
~Epictetus
(Stoic philosopher and a major influence on Ellis)

Rational Emotive Behavior Therapy (REBT) was first introduced by a psychologist Dr Albert Ellis. REBT runs around the concept that humans are not entirely rational creatures and have an innate tendency for irrationality. We think we are rational, but we are like complex computers taking in multiple inputs at a time and producing even more complex outputs at the same time.

While it is (as far as we know) impossible to entirely be rational, Ellis believed that approaching our problems more rationally could have a significant impact on our negative emotions and dysfunctional behaviors*. REBT puts the spotlight on an individual's capacity to unlearn irrational ways and keep on learning rationality. REBT considers that the problems are the A's or Activating factors we spoke about in the earlier stories. And a rational approach means your B or Belief that is logical and realistic. Again, understanding the illogical from the logical is the challenge that REBT throws at us. It sounds very intimidating at first. But when you start to apply the A+B=C regularly, you start identifying even the minute illogical or irrational B's that you carried about your problem (the A).

To sum it up: Dr Ellis, based on his experiences, experiences and deep study, theorized that many of our

113

emotional and behavioral problems spring from basic irrational assumptions or assumptions that are not totally grounded in reality and influence people to act in ways that are inappropriate, unhelpful, or even destructive*.

And he proposed the formula which we now know as A+B=C.

A stands for Activating factors, simply put, irritants/stimuli that trigger your behaviors of anger, sadness, or fear. There can also be triggers that can cause pleasurable emotions like happiness, ecstasy, love, etc.

B stands for belief systems. These consists of two aspects:
  1. Rational or reasonable belief system: which makes you determined and helps you cope effectively in adverse situations.
  2. Irrational or unreasonable belief system: which make you rigid and obstinate in adverse situations leading to failure of your coping mechanism to adverse situations.

C for consequences. There are usually three types of consequences that can seen:
  1. Emotional consequences which consist of unpleasurable or pleasurable emotions
  2. Behavioral consequences which comprise of discomforting or comforting behaviors
  3. Physiological/ physical consequences which include changes in the physiological process in the body- like salivating on thinking of a food that you like *(Fig. 2.1)*, increase in heart rate when you get angry, irritable bowel syndrome when you get fearful, and getting a skin disease like acne, vitiligo, psoriasis, hair thinning, and atopic dermatitis!

My focus is on the unpleasurable or the displeasing emotional consequences and of course the physical ones, because as a dermatologist I see these displeasing emotions leading to skin diseases. A person with skin disease has a range of unpleasurable emotions that manifest the skin disease like acne or psoriasis, and this skin disease has added to their unpleasurable emotions. As for the behavioral consequences, I can take the liberty to say that it is likely that a psychiatrist ends up treating people with behavioral consequences more often than not *(Fig. 5.3)*.

The unpleasurable emotional consequences are the ones that are usually playing hide and seek with us. We know a few emotions like anger, sadness, anxiety, fear, jealousy, greed, etc. But did you know that there are 1700 emotions? For example, every time I am faced with a problem (my A), I experience a negative emotion (my C) that may not be tolerable or is outright torturous. The animated movie *Inside Out* is a perfect example of how we carry our emotions and fail to know them. The character Riley in the movie represents each one of us, where she experiences all five emotions of anger, sadness, disgust, fear, and joy when she moves to San Francisco and has to adjust to new a life. This eleven year old girl called Riley is in us all… Only we haven't learned how to identify her.

As most of us cannot, I couldn't identify my Riley either until a few years ago. And as most of us, I too found myself complaining of how things around us, or people around us are responsible for the frustration or depression, or anger that I experience. But there is more to the understanding of it all than the mere blame game we play.

For an IT guy, his job is responsible for his anger.

For a painter, lack of space would be a reason for his sadness.

For a mother, her kids not eating would be why she gets anxious.

Let's try to analyze these statements.

In the above three cases, the Activating factors (A)/

     McLeod 2015

problems are job, lack of space, and kids respectively. And the emotional Consequences (C) are anger, sadness, and worry respectively.

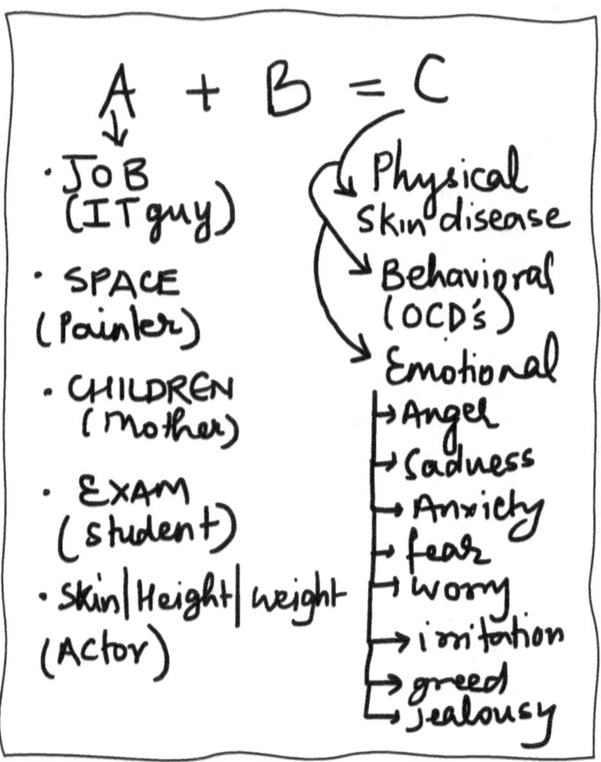

Fig. 12.1

But according to what we know, problems/triggers create negative or unpleasurable emotions. If we were to consider the above statement true, that your problem (A) created your negative emotion (C) then, A would be equal to C.

But look at the formula.

A+B=C.

A = C is not the formula! A is not equal to C.

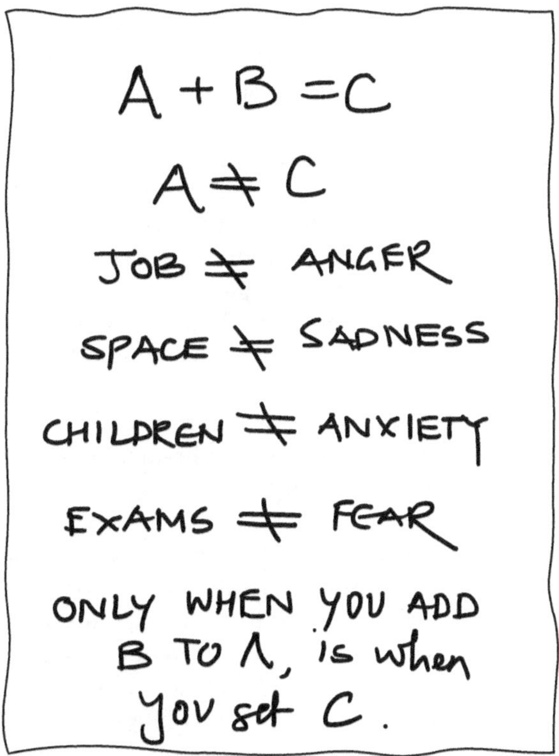

Fig. 12.2

Unless *your* irrational belief system was added to the activating factor, there would be no unpleasurable emotional consequence.

What REBT tries to do is to change your belief systems/ irrational assumptions (about your job, space, and kids) so that you don't feel unpleasurable or harmful emotions. It tries to change your cognitive capacity so that your emotional and physiological tendencies improve through thinking awareness/mindfulness and appropriate behavioral rehearsals. REBT helps your shift from feeling *intolerable* negative emotions to *tolerable* negative emotions to positive pleasing emotions and thereby can manifest positive pleasing physiological outcomes such as disease-free skin.

The first question that does come to mind is why not change the Activating factor (the problem). We could. For the IT guy, he could change jobs. But does changing jobs guarantee better pay or peace of mind? A painter could get a bigger space, but does that guarantee that he would become the next M F Hussain? And as for the mother, changing kids? If that thought came to your mind, you need to get help pronto!

This suggests that even if we had the option to change the activating factors, it did not guarantee a fool-proof method for peace and happiness.

The next question that comes to mind is, why not change the emotion by using distractions? And yes, it is a great way to start. For example, if the IT guy got angry, he could probably go for a walk or listen to some music. If the painter got sad, he could go meet a friend or meditate. If the mother got worried, she could call her mother and get advice. All this will work. But for how long? These tactics will work, till the time the IT guy, painter, and mother are reminded of their respective activating factors/problems. Because the job, space, and kids aren't going anywhere.

As many temporary tactics like music or ice cream help to change emotions instantly, they don't give you long-lasting results.

As I said, you could still agree to disagree with me and say, 'Pradnya, we are going to get better jobs and a bigger space.' Go ahead. I will be happier than you think if you do find long-lasting peace and happiness. But let's say that if you did get a better job but got a boss who was intolerable? If you did get a bigger space, enough to fit a helicopter let us say, and still did not get inspired to paint? And if you didn't get a better job or a bigger space; then the pertinent question would be, how could you improve this state of emotional well-being in the long run? Because, as cheesy as it sounds, life is a marathon and not a sprint that will get better by immediate gratification.

Here is where your B's come into play. Converting illogical or irrational beliefs to rational, logical, and realistic ones is the key to a steady state of mind and thus a steady-state of skin.

The only true authority that you yield in this life is the authority over yourself. It is one true energy that only you can mould and use as per your choice. If you understand this concept of authority and energy, you would be the richest person in the world- and by that, I mean richest in terms of peace and happiness.

The web definition of the word *Belief* is such: 'An acceptance that something exists or is true, especially one without proof'.

Yes, we believe without proof. There are so many examples that can be cited. The 'He said/ She said' game that we play is an example of how we blindly accept most of the information around us. All our beliefs are acquired through nature, nurture, culture, and end up as our signature. As children, due to our limited experiences, nurture and culture through our parents and extended family play an important role in acquiring our beliefs- be it irrational or rational. As we grow older, we start experiencing things in real time helping us to make our existing beliefs obstinate and irrational or helping to unlearn our existing beliefs and make new determined rational ones. We also continuously acquire new beliefs throughout our lives.

Our irrational and obstinate beliefs are not meant to be with us. They do not help us, and on the contrary are harming us. If I asked you to believe something that wasn't true or something that you found difficult to accept- as Aliens existed, would you? If I screamed at the top of my lungs that E T is alive, Steven Spielberg introduced him to me, and he now lives with me, would you believe me? Then why believe your belief system blindly? How do you accept your beliefs/assumptions without proof? Because we are made to believe that that is how the world works. The IT guy is made to believe that jobs are supposed to be hard because everyone around him is complaining of the same. The painter believes that lack of space is a part of his struggle till he becomes an M F Hussain. He further justifies this by saying that not many M F Hussain's are born in a lifetime because he is yet to meet another M F Hussain. The mother is the worst affected I feel. She believes that her young ones are only her responsibility and if they were to lose even hundred grams of weight that would reflect on her ability as a mother because her mother and her mother's mother had set an example so high, that it had to be achieved. The daughter believes that she must get married before she ages so that she can get a good husband. The Actor believes that he must have a certain body type and skin colour to get lead roles. The list is endless. If I asked the IT guy, the painter, the mother, and the daughter to show me proof of what they thought was right- do you think they would be able to provide me even an iota of evidence? No.

Here is another way to simply put a belief system:

Any sentence in which you use with the word *must* or *should* has the potential be a part of an irrational belief system. For example-

I *must not* have acne so that guys like me.

I *must* feed my children before me or else I am a bad mother.

I *must* be perfect in my job or I will lose respect.

Going a step ahead, not all beliefs are irrational or obstinate. To simplify it for you – I divide these B's into those that are workable/rational and those that aren't workable/irrational anymore.

A workable belief would look like the following:
I *would like* score the highest in my class for which I will do my best to achieve it.

Convert this into a non-workable belief and it would look like:
I *must* score at the top of my class, for which I must do my best all the time and at any point of time.

See the difference when a simple word like *must* was replaced with *would-like*? The workable or rational beliefs usually have the words would like. These systems help you run in a determined fashion, enjoying the process of reaching your goal rather than the goal itself. The non-workable beliefs make you rigid, leading you to destructive behavior rather than constructive behavior and take out all the joy of the actual process (process enjoyment). These systems create in you harmful negative emotions even when you turn out second in class!

Then there are workable systems- that which worked for you at a certain point in time and that have now become non-workable.

For example, a twenty-five-year-old girl may have the belief that she *must* get married at twenty-eight. In the years from age twenty-five to twenty-eight, this belief system works for her. But imagine if she weren't married by age twenty-nine? What would happen to her? She could start fearing, worrying, etc. This very system that was working for her between the ages of twenty-five to twenty-nine, now isn't working at all. What would be the next logical thing for her to do? Go marry some Tom Dick Harry just because her belief was such?

Now, don't get me wrong. The above example must have ticked some of you off. Especially if you were today's modern age girl or woman, you couldn't possibly fathom that this thought existed at all. But believe me, there are still millions of girls who live by this thinking and find this thought reassuring. So, is this belief right or wrong? Let me tell you a fact about beliefs- There aren't any wrong ones or right ones, except the ones that involve physical abuse of any sort. Harboring a belief that allows you to get physically abused or physically abuse others is something that even REBT shuns. Outside of this, beliefs are highly subjective. What seems wrong to you, may seem right to someone else. A lot of people start applying subjective beliefs to others and start agonizing over how they are not heard. The fact is that no one is ever going to accept your belief as theirs unless they *want* to accept it. That is why the world is in such discord. Countries are fighting. Racism exists. Climate change is an issue. Malala's are being born. And animals are getting extinct. All because it is difficult to accept subjective beliefs. That's another book for another day. But please do understand that the entire concept of B rests on the fact that a belief is *yours*, and only *you* can change it so that you can improve *your* state of mind.

I understand this can seem overwhelming and it is. When I started being observant of my thoughts, I was constantly confused. But just because something is difficult or confusing do we discard it?

It's one simple formula. One formula that Dr Ellis gave us. Can we not master that?

I guess in a world where we could master complex formulas like $E=MC^2$, A+B=C doesn't seem all so bad, does it?

Now that you are armed with this formula, shall we begin to change your Skin Story?

Here is a list of beliefs (B's) that the Crazy Five had which caused their skin manifestations.

Payal'S beliefs that caused her acne-

- ❖ I MUST look good as I always do *forever*
- ❖ I MUST NOT fall short of making e*veryone* happy
- ❖ I MUST do things to perfection *always*
- ❖ I MUST NOT hear words of criticism *ever*
- ❖ I SHOULD arrange everything in life else
- ❖ I SHOULD give time to my loved ones as and when *they* expect
- ❖ I SHOULD achieve perfection if I am to prove that I am good enough

Varun's beliefs that caused his vitiligo-
- ❖ I MUST be an ideal father *always*
- ❖ My company MUST run perfectly *all the time*
- ❖ I MUST be available to everyone in the family *always*
- ❖ I SHOULD NOT say NO to my family *anytime*
- ❖ I MUST put up a strong face *always*

Mira's beliefs that caused her hair thinning-
- ❖ I MUST be kind to everyone even if it means I am in a bad mood
- ❖ I MUST give preference to family members first
- ❖ I SHOULD be tolerant of my children's tantrums
- ❖ I SHOULD put my career on hold because it would be unfair to my family
- ❖ I MUST not delegate house chores to my family because it would make me look like an uncaring mother or wife

Nihar's beliefs that caused his pigmentation-
- ❖ I MUST take *ideal and perfect* care of things that matter to me
- ❖ I MUST take *total* responsibility for things *all the time*
- ❖ I SHOULD be *totally* attentive to everyone

irrespective of how tired I am
- ❖ I SHOULD fix things immediately or people around me are bound to suffer
- ❖ I MUST NOT stop working because if I do then I will let people down *forever*
- ❖ I MUST NOT hurt anyone at any cost

Mr S's beliefs that caused his psoriasis-
- ❖ I MUST be given justice
- ❖ The world MUST be kinder and nicer *always*
- ❖ Good people MUST NEVER be wronged *ever*
- ❖ People in authority MUST behave in an ethical manner *every time*
- ❖ I MUST get justice because I was wronged

Raghav's beliefs that caused his atopic dermatitis-
- ❖ People MUST NOT be trusted *totally*
- ❖ I MUST be wary of everyone's motives *all the time*
- ❖ I MUST excel in every surgery *always*
- ❖ I SHOULD NOT show my emotions *to anyone*
- ❖ I MUST NOT show my vulnerability because friends or family *will* take advantage

If you observe closely, most of these beliefs finally boil down to self-worth. We attribute our self-worth based on worldly success, validation from others, and the ability to be strong no matter what the situation. Our self-worth is being defined by others unbeknownst to us.

Let's make your list now!

YOUR SKIN STORY

NAME: ♡ _______________

(A)
ACTIVATING
FACTORS FOR YOU

1.

2.

3.

4.

5.

6.

(C)
CONSEQUENCES
YOU FEEL

1.

2.

3.

4.

5.

6.

YOUR BELIEF SYSTEM
ABOUT YOUR ACTIVATING
FACTOR —

1.

2.

3.

4.

5.

6.

YOUR SKIN STORY RETOLD

SHOULDS ⟶ WOULD
MUSTS   LIKES

FOR EXAMPLE :-

I MUST
BE
PERFECT → I WOULD LIKE
IN WHAT   to do my job
I DO   in a manner
           of enjoyment &
           excellence &
           even if I can't
           perform doesn't
           mean I am
           imperfect

I MUST... → I WOULD
              LIKE...

I SHOULD → I WOULD
   ...   LIKE...

If you have made your worksheet – I congratulate you because you took the effort and have come a long way. To explore your thoughts can be a very intimidating process. A Pandora's box waiting to be opened with you not knowing what will come out of it.

If you are struggling with your thoughts – please know that it is a very natural process. There are so many thoughts, both wild and tamed, which are running in our minds that can make it difficult to identify them. One way to streamline them is through meditation, hobby classes, cooking, baking, gardening, trekking, exercise, etc. And once you have identified them, the next step would be to start disputing these identified existing irrational beliefs. Start with asking questions to yourself like:

1. Why do I believe in what I believe?
2. Can I support my belief with objective facts?
3. Is there any proof that my belief is true?
4. Is there proof that this belief is false?
5. How horrible a situation can arise if I don't follow my current belief?
6. Is my belief worth fighting for?
7. Does my belief improve my sense of wellness in real time? Does it benefit others around me and improve their sense of wellness too?

Thought-provoking eh? It is indeed. I remember my early days of acting. I had never gone to acting school, and yet I was working with the greatest theatre director there was- Pandit Satyadev Dubey. One day, after my show, he called out to me and in his baritone husky voice told me one thing that has remained with me ever since. He said, "You will only get better". At that time, I didn't quite understand. But as I continued to act, I understood- rather lived the meaning of this statement. I eventually realized that I could apply this statement to any part of my life. Whoever said practice makes perfect wasn't kidding. And I believe, practice makes it easier to learn and evolve. My 2 cents is that practice isn't about attaining perfection, it's about enjoying the process that leads us to a state of benefit. Because even perfection can be perfected. And anything that can be perfected needs to be rehearsed time and again, over and over, so that we keep getting better at getting perfect only to reach a different level of perfection.

It is time you dealt with all your beliefs that don't serve you anymore. Convert your *must's* into w*ould-like's*. Don't label yourself or others. Avoid putting people in templates. Stop enabling. And last but not the least: keep at it! Because you are not your body or mind. Remember you are your own creation waiting to reveal itself.

All you have to do is tell your skin to heal.

13

Skin science for the skin geek
Know your basics so that there is no basic mein rada

In knowledge lies wisdom and in wisdom lies freedom

~Anon

The skin is an organ. A large one. A visible one. And a beautiful one.

It consists of three layers:

~Epidermis

~Dermis

~Subcutaneous fat

What we see *on* everyone as skin, is the visible epidermis. It is this part of the skin that imparts colour to the person. This is the part that bears all the abuse of the air pollution, cosmetics, creams, treatments, and the sun.

The 3D skin that we perceive on the person is the dermis. Ageing usually starts in this layer by twenty-five years of age and development of fine lines and deep wrinkles occurs in this layer of the skin.

Finally comes the fat; the chubby cheeks that we see on a person. It is the deepest layer and gives body to the skin. It usually starts depleting a little later over the years and as gravity pulls the body down, the fat also starts migrating downward. Thereby giving the famous deepening of the

129

laugh line and formation of the jowl.

Under all this lie the fascia, the muscles along with the major arteries, veins, nerves, and then the bones/ligaments.

Now imagine the absence of the skin…
All the muscle, bones and fascia would be exposed (much like the splayed man of the Bolton's flag in the Game of Thrones) and the body wouldn't have its 'armour' to protect it.
Out of all these layers, the most noteworthy of them all, according to me is the Epidermis.
The epidermis is further divided into 4 more layers-
1-Stratum Corneum (SC)
2-Stratum Granulosum (SG)
3-Stratum Spinulosum (SS)
4- Basale (SB).

Hang on…
I am making it simple- Lets call the layers 1,2,3, and 4.

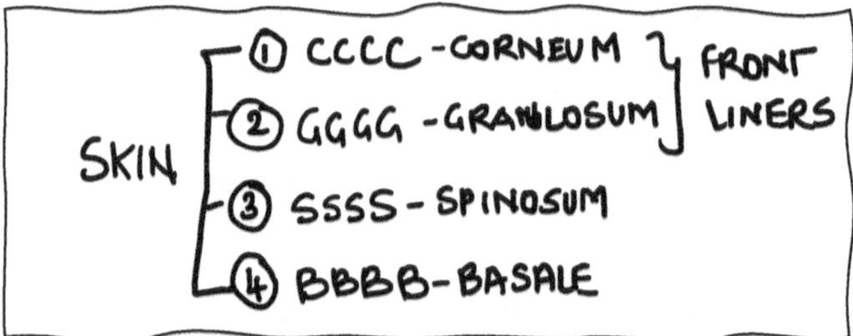

Figure 13.1 Basic layers of skin

Out of these, I personally love layer 1. It is the fro``nt-liner and the bravest warrior of the skin structure and along with the layer 2, becomes a very important defence system of the body.
Layer 1 is considered a biopolymer. It has enough unique properties for us to call it a smart material.

Yes, our skin is a Smart Skin (like the smart phone). That's how intelligent our skin is, rather has been for years, throughout evolution.

Furthermore, layers 1, 2, along with 3 and 4 (total epidermis) keep undergoing renewal. This is called the *epidermal cell turnover'*. It normally takes twenty-nine days for an entire layer of epidermis to replenish itself. Which is why no treatment can work wonders in seven or fifteen days. It needs to be applied for at the least thirty days for a proper visible change.

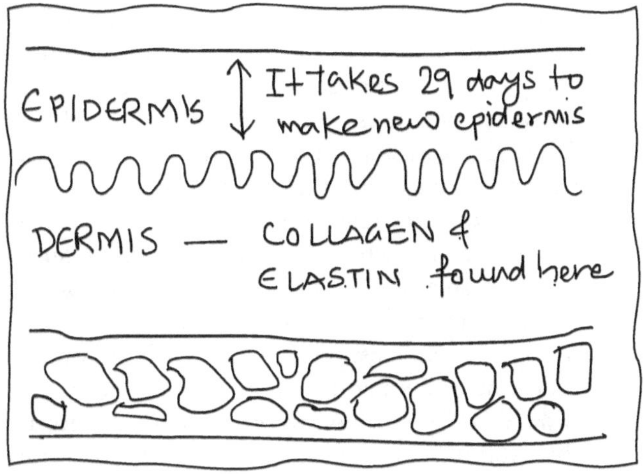

Figure 13.2 Layer 1 of the skin regenerates every 29 days

More on the Smartness of our skin:
It works passively and actively.
Passively the Smart Skin acts like Iron man's Jarvis:

    a.   Our Jarvis selectively lets particles in, for example— it will let in creams but not let in viruses. So, if any ill person sneezed on you, you would have warrior 1 and 2 working for you, fencing all the viruses and bacteria.

    b.   It heals it self- How many times have you really had

to go to a Dermatologist for a cut or bruise? In that case, everyone in Games of Thrones, with their cuts and bruises would be in the hospital forever!

c. It attaches itself to the body and ensures stability in structure. Imagine if the skin slipped off like lose pants every time you moved? We'd all be covered with clothes pins trying to hold the skin together.

And so smart is our skin that all this is being done effortlessly.

Actively our Smart Skin acts like Iron Man:

a. Senses ambient humidity changes. Lack of this smart feature would entail to heat strokes in summer and gangrenous fingers in the winter. Because you sense temperatures, you can decide your clothing (there are exceptions of course: the fashion industry, where ambience ain't mattering evaaa).

b. Uses its own feedback system. If it doesn't like the cream you are using, it will speak to you. Consider the red rash as a s**** y** language of the skin. You would be compelled to stop the cream.

c. Makes a useful response as is seen in a condition called neurodermatitis, or in laymen terms, *Stress Induced Itching*. Imagine when stressed you got into the habit of scratching, the skin would simple adapt and respond by thickening the skin, instead of thinning. So that you wouldn't scratch yourself to the bone.

d. Another example, particularly layer 1 + 2, are effective in increasing the oil secretion leading to a softer, glowing, and well hydrated skin in a dry weather.

e. And like it detects changes in humidity, the skin also has various other receptors (receiving stations) like
- Thermoreceptors for heat and cold
- Nociceptor for pain and
- Mechanoreceptors for mechanical changes

These receptors are responsible for transmitting the outside signals to the spinal cord, and then to the brain. The brain then responds to these signals, which in turn influence the stress responses in the skin.

And here is where the Brain (mind) – Skin link comes in. Remember when I quoted 'what you think you become'? The brain also responds to various harmful thoughts and through the vicious Thought – Disease loop *(Fig. 5.3)* creates the skin disease. When you are in distress and overworked, the cortisol levels go for a toss *(Fig. 6.2)*. It is these levels that act on the skin and lead to variety of skin conditions like adult acne, psoriasis, vitiligo etc.

Furthermore, not taking care of your body (sleeping late, not eating on time and not exercising) can also lead to raised cortisol level and raised insulin levels, thus leading to conditions like acne, psoriasis, vitiligo etc.

So, you are not only what you think, you are also what you eat and how you sleep too!

Moving ahead- The dermis holds the collagen and elastin and a part of the blood vessels. Ageing starts here. The blushing of the skin when you see someone attractive happens here. A lot of deep skin conditions like lupus or vasculitis occur here. Like epidermis has a turnover rate, the dermis doesn't. Which means, by the time you reach twenty-five years of age, the collagen stops forming, making ageing permanent. So, remember that no cream can cause reversal of ageing: One, because the smart skin wouldn't allow the cream to penetrate so deep, and two, because collagen rejuvenation is a far more complicated process (remember we dermatologists exist for a reason).

The last layer, the subcutaneous fat, I believe is the cute layer. But many fear the word fat, thanks to the fads about food and self-image that exist. But this is the layer that makes your cheeks look cute and along with the deeper fat in your body, makes your butt look cute too. Like the dermis, the cells of the fatty layer also undergo death and downward migration due to gravity. This layer supports the overlying dermis, and as it undergoes shriveling, the skin on top starts to lose its contour. So, au contraire to all those fads, some fat in the form of padding is needed for you to have a youthful body. Else you would look like a lemon on a stick. Who would want that eh? Plus, this fat helps you keep warm in a chilly weather by a process called as thermogenesis. Fat, in the right amount, is fantastic I say!

To sum up, you wouldn't exist without your skin. It was, is and continues to be your life saver, appearance wise and health wise. We now know how it acts in tandem with the other organs like the brain and can protect you as well as break you. It is one of the most beautiful organs of a wonder called the human body and I am proud to have studied it in depth. I am also humbled to have been able to pass on whatever information I have about it to you. As a dermatologist, I hope you use this information and never forget the one truth: that your healing lies within you. It lies in how you use the information you have received thus far. I hope this information sets you free from your skin disease. I hope you glow as you were meant to.

14

Prescription Stories

My words of prescriptive medicinal gyaan

*The natural healing force within each of us is the greatest force in
getting well*
~ Hippocrates

I certainly believe in prescriptive medicine. But I also believe in the power of the body to heal itself. Creams matter, but what matters more is *how* you use them. Here are my instructions given to the Crazy Five and Mr S for your understanding and clarity on how just applying a cream isn't all that is to be done. Applying creams with mindfulness and changing skincare habits, both need to be done simultaneously.

Payal's Acne

Acne vulgaris or pimples as we know, is of 4 types: Comedones(black/whiteheads), Papules (red bumps), Pustules (white pus filled bumps), Cysts (large hard tender bumps).

In Payal's case she was suffering from blackheads, whiteheads, and papules of various sizes predominantly in the mandibular area or jaw line. Mandibular acne is most likely due to hormonal imbalances and can be painful and non-remitting, requiring long term treatment.

I started Payal on an antibiotic gel in the day time and a retinoid based cream at night.

She was to wash her face only twice a day and the other times, if the face got oily, she was to dab off this excess oil with a tissue paper. Retinoids make the skin dry. If Payal continued to wash face as she was, then it would be difficult to know if the dryness was due to washing of the face, the face wash or the retinoid.

I also added an anti-dandruff shampoo because acne can sometimes be associated with dandruff as well.

She was to follow the prescription for the next 15 days! Because follow-ups are required. Remember the skin sheds off every twenty-nine days. The initial phase of treatments needs active monitoring to improve the overall outcomes. There is no magical cream that can magically remove your acne in magical time! Dermatologists function in real time! So follow-up and show up!

Sleeping at 10 pm to regularise her melatonin levels was imperative.

Waking up in the morning and breaking her fast with a fruit was advised.

Regular meals at the right time ensured that her brain and body got the necessary fuel to burn and nutrition to thrive on, thereby improving her anti-oxidative repairs.

Exercising to regularise her insulin levels would help her reduce her body fat (not weight!) and her overall fitness.

Treatments that I planned for her:
1. Active acne phase:
-   Three chemical peels fifteen days apart.
-   Once the new acne stopped and old lesions flattened: Intense Pulse Light therapy with chemical peels three sessions fifteen days apart
2. Maintenance phase when no new lesions appeared and what remained were scars and pigmentation:
-   Three sessions of Carbon dioxide fractional laser and Platelet Rich Plasma therapy (PRP). Both would help stimulate the dermal collagen and help smoothen the scar appearance.

Varun's Vitiligo

Vitiligo is a type of leukoderma. That means that all forms of vitiligo are leucoderma's, but not all leukoderma's are vitiligo. Basically, you don't need to panic every time you see a white patch. Keep calm and visit a dermatologist!

Vitiligo is an autoimmune skin disease where the defence cells start killing the melanocytes (colour producing cells).

There can be various types of vitiligo based on where the patches are seen. In Varun's case, he had lip-tip vitiligo where the patches are seen predominantly on the lips and tips of finger, toes, and private parts.

Vitiligo is also categorized as stable (no new patches are seen in six months), and unstable (new patches are appearing at slow or fast pace).

Varun had stable vitiligo by the time I met him and so I decided not to start him on oral steroids.

I started him oral tablets that promote repigmentation. He was to take the tablet two hours before sun exposure and expose himself to UV rays of the evening 4 pm sun for ten minutes.

I also added topical steroid creams to help aid the process of forming colour.

Lifestyles changes were important. He agreed to sleep at 11 pm instead of 1 am. I keep saying this to all my patients, start with baby steps. One cannot change lifestyles overnight. Instead of getting overwhelmed, start slowly but be perseverant and continue to improve your timings.

He also agreed to eat more fruits and eat clean i.e., no processed or preserved foods to reduce the oxidative damage that was happening in his skin.

He was all set to start cycling as well.

I was to see him after fifteen days.

Mira's Hair Thinning

Hair thinning in women has become a common occurrence. Men have been known to suffer patterned baldness from long before. In case of women, this patterned thinning seems to be on the rise, with girls as young as eighteen showing thinned out hair.

Hair growth solutions like minoxidil work very well and I started her on the same.

Minoxidil needs to be used regularly. She needed to apply it regularly on her scalp at night for 8 months in a row. This would then be followed by tapering the number of applications in a week to three or four times in allow to maintain the hair growth that was achieved.

Caffeine based hair shampoo was started.

Washing of hair and hair fall are not corelated. Many of my patients complain of how the hair started to fall 'more' after shampooing and especially after the use of a conditioner. If shampoos and conditioners caused balding, then the whole world would be bald by now! But new shampoos with various technologies continue to pour into the market!

Both shampoos and conditioners are to be used together. The shampoo cleans the scalp and the conditioner will maintain the structure of the hair by closing the cuticles that opened during shampooing.

I asked her to wash her scalp three times a week.

Again, there is no rule to washing your hair. If you think your scalp is oily, then feel free to wash it as much as every day. If you think it is dry, then you could probably wash every three days. But again, learn to understand the feedback from your scalp and then decide if you would want to wash or not! Your skin and hair talk to you. Listen.

Mira always woke up at 6 am owing to her children's school, but she vowed to inculcate healthy sleeping patterns in her family. The kids would now be put to bed by 8.30 pm and the elders would aim to go to sleep at a healthy hour.

She was going to start her singing and along with that she would add dancing as a form of fitness.

Mira was going to sing and dance herself to fitness and great hair.

A follow up of three months was advised. As in the case of hair, it takes at least three months for new hair growth to be seen on the scalp. Therefore remember, hair care is a slow process. Beware of quick fix solutions.

Nihar's facial pigmentation

Facial acanthosis commonly occurs on the forehead, around eyes, and cheeks. The skin looks dull and dark with enlarged pores. Even the skin on the neck and the underarms can thicken leading to a condition called pseudoacanthosis nigricans.

This happens due to insulin resistance and so the primary treatment lies in an immediate change in lifestyle.

Nihar was sleeping by 9 pm and was usually up at 5 am. But his eating, though was fresh and clean, straight from the farm, it wasn't on time. He was erratic in his habits. Regularizing the time was needed.

He would start active counselling and learn how to let-go of things.

I still started him on a 50 SPF physical sunscreen owing to extended time in the sun. Now, a sunscreen needs to be applied thirty minutes before sun exposure, every three hours. It needs thirty minutes to bind to the skin surface for it to reflect light and work efficiently. Nihar would now be also using a good broad brimmed hat. The *Gavaskar Topi* as we called it.

I also started him on a glycolic acid cream with a moisturiser and asked to see him after fifteen days.

He said since Saraswati his cow had fallen in love with me, that I come over to the farm. Who can resist some pure unconditional love eh?

Mr S's psoriasis

Psoriasis is also an autoimmune disease. It can disappear in three months or can last up to thirty months. All depending on how the treatments are happening and how the lifestyle is being modified.

I started him on topical steroid creams, moisturizers, and some anti-itching tablets.

The oral methotrexate drug, which is primarily used in cancer, is used in the treatment in psoriasis. And I decided to use this in his case. The reason an anti-cancer drug is used is because, the skin cells are rapidly multiplying in psoriasis, as are the cancer cells in any cancer. Methotrexate reduces the speed of multiplication of the skin cells thereby leading to reduction of the scales and clearing the patches. Weekly doses are given and with strict blood monitoring, I started him on the same.

He was to see me after fifteen days with his journal, where he would be jotting down all those harmful thoughts that he would like to change.

Mr and Mrs S both would change their lifestyles by decreasing their *Gulab Jams* and increasing their apples.

They knew that an apple a day would keep the skin doctor away.

Raghav's atopic dermatitis

Raghav and I would meet after fifteen days. I had started him on steroid creams and it was decided that he would use powder free surgical gloves while operating. I also insisted that he carry a moisturiser in his bag to be used as often as can be.

The other basic instructions that I give all patients of atopic dermatitis are:
- Apply coconut oil 5 minutes before bathing
- Use lukewarm water or tap water for bathing
- Avoid showers and prefer bucket baths instead
- Use pH balanced soaps with minimal lathering
- Apply a good moisturizer immediately after bath on damp skin

Patients with atopic dermatitis tend to overclean themselves. They think the itch is due to dirt. I have seen patients who wash hands as much as twenty times a day. This only reduces the Natural Moisturising Factor (NMF) of your skin and further breaks the skin barrier by changing the pH balance. So all you frequent washers and bathers… stop. Understand the need of your skin and then decide if you need to wash or bathe.

Atopic dermatitis has high association with stress. Patches of rough, red, and thick skin were seen on Raghav's hands and his neck when I had met him. He agreed to work on writing down all the day's events and trying to find if his negative thoughts were aggravating the itch.

His next move: To learn how to make time for himself. Surprisingly, he was going to pick up photography… and click the Crazy Five on Nihar's farm, in the backdrop of Mira's melodious voice, after Varun sold off his third company and before Payal got married.

P.S. He did shoot. We all featured as models with healed and glowing skins.

References and reads for the skin geek

1.   Acne and Stress: Impact of Catecholamines on Cutibacterium acne

2.   New insights into skin structure: scratching the surface- Gopinathan K Menon.

3.   Brain-Skin Connection: Stress, Inflammation and Skin Aging Ying Chen* and John Lyga .

4.   Skin as a Container Mediating Primary Self-Other Relationships: An Exploration of the Psychological Function of Skin Disorders by Katie Banks

5.   A Classification of psychological distress for use in primary care settings. David Goldberg Mental Illness Research Unit, University of Manchester, U.K.

6.   A tentative classification of psychological factors in the etiology of skin diseases. Robert Brandt, M.D.

7.   Somatization and the Recognition of Depression and Anxiety in Primary Care Laurence J. Kirmayer, M.D., James M. Robbins, Ph.D., Michael Dworkind, M.D., and Mark J. Yaffe, M.D.

8.   Somatization: The Concept and Its Clinical Application Z.J. Lipowski, M.D., F.R.C.P.(C)

9.   Sonic stress as one of the cardinal risk factors for atherosclerosis Reibun Kambara, Yoshihiro Fukuo, Kazumasa Hada, Takashi Hasegawa and Akiro Terashi. The Second Department of Internal Medicine, Nippon Medical School Research Institute of Gerontology , Nippon Medical School. J. Nippon Med. Sch., Vol. 60, No. 1 (1993)

10. Environmental influences on skin aging and ethnic-specific manifestations Andrea Vierkötter & Jean Krutmann.

11. Effects of Relaxation Therapy and Hypnotizability in Chronic Urticaria Carolyn L. Shertzer, PhD, Donald P. Lookingbill, MD. Arch Dermatol 1987;123:913-916)

12. Skin in the Game by Frank Summers.

13. Indications for a 'brain–hair follicle axis (BHA)': inhibition of keratinocyte proliferation and up-regulation of keratinocyte apoptosis in telogen hair follicles by stress and substance. P Petra, Clara Arck, Bori Handjiski, Evelin Hagen, Ricarda Joachim, Burghard F. Klapp, Ralf.

ABOUT THE AUTHOR

Dr Pradnya Manwatkar is a Dermatologist by choice, Actor by chance, Painter by night and Writer by day!

As a dermatologist, she provides a variety of dermatology & cosmetic dermatology treatments with the firm belief that skin issues need active counselling, more than just medication. She completed her training hours in REBT- Rational Emotive Behaviour Therapy, and actively counsels her patients to ensure better treatment outcomes. The awareness about The Brain- Skin Link and Emodermatology is what she is working towards creating.

As an actor, she has TV commercials to her name, along with plays, series, and films in Hindi and English.

Her love for writing has finally led to the culmination of this book.

And as for painting, an occasional stroke of watercolour keeps her skin stress free.